C.E.H.J. Verhoef

THE BATTLE FOR GINKEL HEATH NEAR EDE
17 & 18 September 1944

Translated from the original Dutch text by Hanjo Braakman.

2003 Aspekt

Front cover photographs: The King's Own Scottish Borderers cap badge (Courtesy R.N. Sigmond), landing of paratroopers and Airborne Monument on Ginkel Heath (Photo: author).

The Battle for Ginkel Heath near Ede – 17 & 18 September 1944
© 2003 C.E.H.J. Verhoef
© 2003 Uitgeverij Aspekt bv
Amersfoortsestraat 27, 3769 AD Soesterberg, The Netherlands
aspekt@knoware.nl
www.uitgeverijaspekt.nl
Cover design: Peter Koch
Inside: Van Swieten & Partner, Nieuwegein, The Netherlands
ISBN: 90-5911-386-1

Contents

Introduction

Even fifty-nine years after the actual fighting the Battle of Arnhem still represents a most telling defeat for a great many people. The fierce and bloody fighting for the bridge across the river Rhine near the capital of the Dutch province of Gelderland is perhaps one of the best-known episodes in the history of the Second World War. Scores of books, newspaper articles, documentary and even some feature films have been dedicated to the planning and execution of Field Marshal Montgomery's plan of attack. As the liberation of the part of Holland above the great rivers only seemed a matter of time, its tragic outcome had traumatic consequences for all who participated in the fighting. Tragically, the crossing of the Rhine appeared to be 'a bridge too far'.

The heroic and valiant actions by the British and Polish airborne troops at the Arnhem road bridge and in the Oosterbeek perimeter, which latter acted as bridgehead round the headquarters of the 1st British Airborne Division at Hotel Hartenstein, are well known. Less well known is what happened during the first days of Operation Market Garden at Ginkel Heath, east of Ede, where nearly two thousand British parachutists landed on 18 September 1944.

To keep the memory of these momentous events on the heath alive, it is commemorated each year by the landing of a few WWII veterans and of paratroopers of the present British army.

However, many of the spectators are not familiar with the specific events that took place in that part of the Veluwe region during those September days. The landing of the 4th Parachute Brigade was only part of all military activities on and around Ginkel Heath and took only nine minutes. The fact that the arrival of the brigade was preceded by almost twenty-four hours of fierce fighting is practically unknown to visitors to these annual landings.

In most written and oral reports on the Battle of Arnhem none or hardly any attention is paid to this episode. In this book the fighting on the heath near Ede plays a central role. Issues as 'The allied strategy after the Normandy landings', 'Eisenhower's Decision', 'The course of events in Arnhem and Oosterbeek', 'Was the Battle of Arnhem betrayed?' and 'The reasons for defeat' are mentioned in both the text and the notes, but only when necessary for the broader picture and understanding of the fighting that took place on Ginkel Heath.

For the same reason emphasis is laid on the actions of the British army units that were involved in the Battle for Ginkel Heath, i.e. the 7th Battalion The King's Own Scottish Borderers (7 KOSB), 4th Parachute Brigade, 21st Independent Parachute Company and 133 Parachute Field Ambulance. This also applies to the forces deployed by the Germans viz. *Luftwaffe* (Air Force) personnel and troops of the *4. SS Panzer Grenadier Ausbildungs – und Ersatz Bataillon* (Trainings and Reserve Battalion) billeted in Simon Stevin barracks in Ede, the *20. SS Schiffs-Stamm-Abteilung* (a naval manning unit) from Maurits and Johan Willem Friso barracks in Ede, the *SS Wach-Bataillon 3* (carried out guard duties at the Amersfoort concentration camp)[1], two artillery batteries from Wageningen, one battalion of the *Sicherungsregiment 42* (assigned to guard duties) and one *SS Ausbildungs Bataillon* (Trainingsbattalion).

1. Allied Strategy after the Normandy Landings.

Early in the morning of 6 June 1944 allied forces landed on the coast of Normandy. The attack on Hitler's *Festung Europa* (Fortress Europe) had finally started. After heavy fighting the Allies succeeded in establishing a bridgehead and two months later they broke through the German defences. Approximately one million allied soldiers quickly spread out over the northern and eastern parts of France. On 25 August Paris was liberated, followed by Liège on 2 September, Brussels on the 3rd and Antwerp a day later. During the last six days some army units covered a distance of over 400 kilometres.

However, on 10 September the allied advance came to a halt at the Meuse-Escaut Canal in the northern part of Belgium.

The crucial strategic question of how to proceed from there was heavily disputed within the allied high command. The American General Eisenhower, the Supreme Allied Commander, favoured a 'broad front strategy', which included a number of forward moves by all his armies towards the river Rhine. From there the heart of the German hinterland was to be attacked along the broadest possible front.

The British Field Marshal Montgomery, commanding 21st Army Group, however, pressed hard for a 'small front strategy'. According to him the Germans were almost totally defeated and a concentrated attack from northern Belgium into Holland would enable the Allies to reach the bridge at Arnhem. Such an attack would take the Germans by surprise because they were expecting an allied offen-

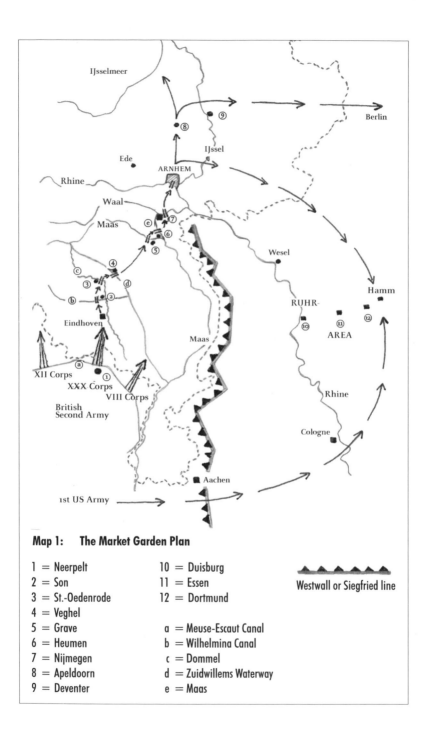

Map 1: The Market Garden Plan

1 = Neerpelt	10 = Duisburg
2 = Son	11 = Essen
3 = St.-Oedenrode	12 = Dortmund
4 = Veghel	
5 = Grave	a = Meuse-Escaut Canal
6 = Heumen	b = Wilhelmina Canal
7 = Nijmegen	c = Dommel
8 = Apeldoorn	d = Zuidwillems Waterway
9 = Deventer	e = Maas

Westwall or Siegfried line

sive towards the Rhine in Germany and he therefore opted for another strategy.[1] He wanted to bypass the *Westwall* or Siegfried Line, which ran from Cleves to Switzerland and which the Germans had constructed to defend their western border.

In his *Memoirs* Montgomery called his strategy 'a reverse *Von Schlieffen* plan'. He wanted to do the same with the Siegfried Line as the Germans had done with the line of defence along the French eastern border stretching from Luxemburg to Basle during the First World War and in 1940 when they had thrusted ahead north of these fortifications into northwestern France.[2]
After having taken Arnhem the Allies would branch off to the right and take the Ruhr area and advance on Berlin. In his view the war could thus be ended before Christmas 1944 (see map no. 1).

Eisenhower was opposed to such a 'spearhead attack'.[3] Early September the supply of the forces could hardly keep up with the allied advance. According to the timetable of Operation Overlord the conquest of Western-Europe would take the allied forces to a line between Dieppe and Paris after approximately four months, i.e. D + 120.

However, the advance had progressed so fast that the southern border of Holland was reached after three months only viz. D + 90.[4] Antwerp and the Channel ports were still occupied by the Germans and could therefore not be used to bring in the necessary supplies and reinforcements. The French railway system and airfields were badly damaged by allied bomber attacks and sabotage actions by the resistance movement and could therefore also not be used to resupply the allied forces. All necessary goods for the conduct of war were landed at the artificial harbours off the Normandy coast and had to be transported over a distance of more than 375 miles to the frontline and consequently this took a lot of improvisation. Each lorry was driven for at least twenty hours each day and only stopped for loading, unloading and maintenance.

The rapid advance also meant great problems for Montgomery's 21st Army Group. Over fourteen hundred British three ton lorries,

28 August 1944. Eisenhower (left) and Montgomery leave 21st Army Group HQ, where they have privately discussed the 'Allied strategy north of the river Seine'. (*Montgomery, Memoires,* p.275)

the backbone of Montgomery's chain of supply, could not be used because of defective engines. Besides a shortage of petrol the tanks of the British Second Army of General Dempsey were for the most part almost worn out.[5] For two weeks some British units only had canned food, cheese and bread taken from seized German depots because their own supplies could not reach them in sufficient quantities.[6]

In case of an allied advance over a small front the Germans in Eisenhower's view would also be able to squeeze the supply lines of Montgomery's forces. In order to prevent this from happening and to protect the flanks one division after the other should have to be left behind with the major disadvantage of gradually slowing down the advance. Eisenhower was aware of the fact that the Germans still had a considerable number of reserve troops at their disposal in the central part of their country. In his memoirs titled *Crusade in Europe* he wrote that the enemy would immediately repel each 'pencillike thrust' into the heartland of Germany.[7]

After much haggling between the two commanders Eisenhower finally agreed to a small-scale operation to form a bridgehead across the Rhine at Arnhem [8], which was meant as 'a foothold opening the door to the German heartland'.[9]

It was code-named Operation Market Garden, which started on 17 September 1944 and would end in the Battle of Arnhem.

Operation Market Garden

Montgomery's plan consisted of two parts. Operation Market was the seizure of eight bridges over the waterways between the Belgian border and Arnhem by the First Allied Airborne Army. Operation Garden was to be the ground attack by the British Second Army from its positions on the Meuse-Escaut Canal in Belgium towards the IJsselmeer.

Operation Market turned out to be 'the biggest air armada in history'.[10] The allied air forces lifted a total of 20,190 paratroopers,

5,230 tons of equipment and supplies, 1,927 vehicles and 568 guns, both light and heavy, some of which weighed more than two tons each. All this was dropped behind the German lines between Eindhoven and Wolfheze. Moreover, a number of 13,781 men were carried to the battle zone by gliders.[11]

The task of the First Allied Airborne Army was both difficult and spectacular. The three divisions of this force each had a different assignment and were to operate up to sixty-five miles behind the German lines in occupied Holland. The 101st US Airborne Division, the 'Screaming Eagles', was to take the bridges over the Wilhelmina Canal near Son, over the river Dommel near Sint Oedenrode and over the Zuidwillems Waterway and the river Aa near Veghel. The 82nd US Airborne Division, the 'All American', was to be dropped near Grave, Groesbeek and Overasselt and to take the bridges over the river Maas near Grave, over the Maas-Waal Canal near Heumen and over the river Waal at Nijmegen. The road bridge over the river Rhine at Arnhem was assigned to the 1st British Airborne Division and the 1st Polish Independent Parachute Brigade Group.

By means of this 'carpet', laid out by the Airborne Divisions after taking all these bridges, XXX Corps of the British Second Army consisting of the tanks of the Guards Armoured Division, the 8th Armoured Brigade, the infantry of the 43rd (Wessex) and the 50th (Northumbrian) Divisions and covered on the flanks by both VIII and XII Corps, was to reach the Arnhem road bridge within forty-eight hours. The Arnhem bridgehead would give Montgomery the opportunity to push on to the Ruhr area, the centre of the German steel and war industry and ultimately to Berlin, the capital of Nazi-Germany.[12]

None of the other allied army commanders was very enthusiastic when being informed about Montgomery's plan. One of the many critics was General Dempsey, the commander of the British Second Army. Already on 10 September he made it clear to Montgomery that the stiff German opposition in northern Belgium together with

Generals Bradley (left) of the 12th US Army Group and Dempsey (right) of the British Second Army were both critics of Montgomery's plan.   (PHOTO: COURTESY OF THE IMPERIAL WAR MUSEUM, LONDON)

reports on German troop movements were a bad omen.

He had also received reports from the Dutch resistance about the presence of German tanks in the vicinity of Arnhem. Moreover, between Neerpelt and Arnhem his troops were to advance along a single two-lane road, which was just wide enough for one tank.

On 10 September Dempsey suggested to Montgomery to change the plan of attack and instead of advancing north towards Arnhem to head for Venlo and cross the river Rhine together with the Americans at Wesel. Montgomery turned this down because of the presence of many anti-aircraft guns in and around the Ruhr area. The Field Marshal also had another reason. On 8 September he had received reports that the first V-2's (V standing for *Vergeltungswaffe* which means 'weapon of retaliation') were launched from bases in Holland towards London. In his *Memoirs* Montgomery wrote: 'As far as I am concerned this fact finally decided the direction of the offensive.'[13]

However, it appears that he did not want to change his plans at all and only used the argument of the V-2's to push his original plan through. There is no evidence whatsoever that either the British government or the British Supreme Command put any pressure on Montgomery to advance into Holland because of the presence of the V-2 rockets. There was no necessity to change the military strategy for this reason.[14]

Montgomery's optimism knew no limits. He saw the great stride forward to Arnhem as the beginning of a 'goldrush'. At the end Berlin was waiting. In a letter dated 15 September to his friend Grigg the Field Marshal wrote: 'From 17th September onwards things should be very exciting and when we have the Ruhr I do not fancy the end (of the war) will be far off.'[15]

2. Sunday, 17 September 1944: D-Day

Operation Market Garden started on the night of 16 and in the early morning of 17 September with bombing raids by Lancasters and Mosquitoes from RAF Bomber Command. Several airfields in Holland and the western part of Germany such as Leeuwarden, Steenwijk-Havelte, Eindhoven, Hopsten and Salzbergen were heavily damaged.[1] Early on the 17th these bombardments were continued by fighter-bombers, Thunderbolts, Lightnings and Mustangs, whose targets were coastal batteries and anti-aircraft guns (the notorious Flak which stands for *Flugzeug Abwehr Kanone*) at Moerdijk and Eindhoven. Visibility was excellent and there was no opposition from the German air force. Flak was negligible except in the area round Arnhem, which in a report from the allied air forces was described as 'moderate but inaccurate'.[2]

Later that same morning hostile troop concentrations, coastal defences, railway junctions, ferries and roads in the Westerschelde and Walcheren areas were hit as well as barracks and anti-aircraft batteries in Nijmegen, Cleves, Arnhem and Ede.

Around noon thirteen Boston and thirty Mitchell bombers of the 2nd Tactical Air Force appeared in the skies above Ede and their 281-fivehundred pound bombs caused a massive destruction. In the daily report of the Allied Expeditionary Air Force (AEAF) the result was qualified as 'very good' although this is subject to a lot of discussion.[3]

The Enka rayon works, Ede-Wageningen station and adjacent buildings and barracks were hit. In the southern part of Ede the

On 17 September 1944 the Roman-Catholic Church on Stationsweg at Ede was hit. Afterwards the remnants of the church were burned down by the Germans. (PHOTO: MUNICIPAL ARCHIVES, EDE, NO. 5323)

Twijnstraat was practically obliterated. The Parkweg, Padberglaan, Laan 1933, the Barbara Foundation and Hotel Terminus were also badly damaged. About one hour later a number of bombs hit the centre of the village and a total of 1,261 houses were damaged of which 165 badly and forty-six houses were completely destroyed. The Roman Catholic Church on Stationsweg was reduced to rubble and there were sixty-four casualties among the civilian population.[4] The cultural centre De Reehorst functioned as an emergency hospital.

In his *Gefechtsbericht* (war diary) 1st Lieutenant Labahn, the German *Ortskommandant* (town-major) in Ede, who was also in charge of Simon Stevin barracks, reported that at 12.15 hours these barracks were hit, which resulted in eleven killed and thirty wounded. A little later an air raid on Beeckman barracks caused about eleven dead and sixteen wounded.[5]

From a military point of view these bombardments can be considered more or less a failure. The original plan was to knock out the Ede-Wageningen railway junction, but this remained intact. Of the military targets only some barracks and schools in the village, where German soldiers were billeted, were hit. The damage to these barracks was limited and only a few warehouses and some stables, vehicle sheds and a guardroom were hit. These air raids had little impact on the enemy's resistance.

The air attacks were executed under perfect weather conditions and without any serious anti-aircraft activities, but still resulted in many unnecessary casualties. Wageningen and Wolfheze were also hit but, as in Ede, there were a lot of civilians killed and wounded. Contrary to the AEAF, the retired Lieutenant Colonel from Ede, Mr Boeree, spoke of an 'unnecessary bombardment'.[6]

The Germans set fire to the remains of the damaged barracks as well as to some other buildings in Ede. A number of inhabitants managed to enter the barracks grounds just in time to take part of the supplies, such as shoes, blankets and rucksacks.

THE TAKE-OFF OF THE BIGGEST AIR ARMADA IN HISTORY

After the early morning mist had lifted the signal was given for the start of the biggest airborne operation in history. The first to depart from Fairford airfield in the south of England was a detachment of Pathfinders. Twelve Stirlings carried six officers and 180 men of the 21st Independent Parachute Company under the command of Major B.A. Wilson. Their task was to mark the various Drop Zones (DZ for parachutists and supplies) and Landing Zones (LZ for gliders) west of Arnhem (see map no. 2) with beacons ('Eureka' radio beacons), smoke canisters and large white panels. These were laid out to indicate the code letters of the DZs and LZs whilst the letter 'T' denoted the wind direction.

The Pathfinders took to their task full of confidence. Convinced that the war was nearly over most of them had brought brass and shoe polish in order to 'smarten up for liberation parties and the glorious entry into Germany'. Their commanding officer carried bottles of scotch, gin and sherry as a treat for members of the Dutch resistance.[7]

Operation Market had begun.

After the departure of the Pathfinders the biggest air fleet ever and comprising more than 3,500 aircraft took off at 09.45 hours from

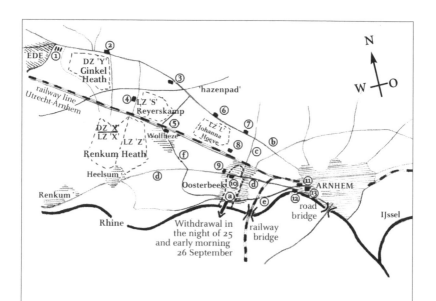

Map 2:   DZs and LZs on 17 and 18 September 1944.

Drop and Landing Zones:

	17 September	DZ 'X'
		LZ 'S'
		LZ 'Z'
	18 September:	DZ 'Y'
		LZ 'X'
		LZ 'S'
		LZ 'L'

a = Perimeter Oosterbeek
b = Amsterdamseweg
c = Dreijenseweg
d = Utrechtseweg
e = Benedendorpsweg/Klingelbeekseweg/
     Hulkesteinseweg
f = Wolfhezerweg

1 = Simon Stevin barracks
2 = Zuid Ginkel Café
3 = Planken Wambuis Café
4 = De Buunderkamp Hotel
5 = Wolfheze railway station
6 = Schweizer Höhe
7 = Pumpingstation Arnhem waterworks
8 = Johannahoeve Farm
9 = De Bilderberg Hotel
10 = Hartenstein Hotel
11 = St. Elisabeth's Hospital
12 = Rijnpaviljoen Hotel
13 = Municipal Museum

twenty-four airfields in southern and eastern England.

Approximately 1,500 troop carriers with paratroopers and nearly five hundred tug planes pulling a glider each on a nearly one hundred metre long cable, partly loaded with jeeps, supplies and anti-tank guns and partly carrying troops headed for the Dutch coast.[8] The air armada was escorted by hundreds of fighters, which included a large number of Spitfires. The transport planes and gliders carried the majority of the three airborne divisions to their landing areas, viz. most of the 101st US Airborne Division to Son and Veghel, part of the 82nd US Airborne Division to Grave, Groesbeek and Overasselt and the vanguard of the 1st British Airborne Division to their dropping and landing zones west of Arnhem.

The airborne troops were relieved to finally go into action. After sixteen previous cancellations Market Garden was to be the seventeenth plan to bring the First Allied Airborne Army into battle.

Because of the shortage of aircraft and gliders the commander of the 1st Allied Airborne Army, the American Lieutenant General Brereton, had decided to fly his troops to their destination in a number of lifts. The 1st British Airborne Division under the command of Major General Urquhart and totalling 8,969 officers and other ranks plus 1,126 glider pilots, was to go across in three lifts.[9] Because of the above mentioned lack of planes the Supreme Command could have decided to execute two lifts per day. However, Brereton insisted that his pilots would only fly one sortie per day in order to prevent them of getting too exhausted. By doing so the ground crews would also be able to check and service the aircraft at their home bases and prepare them for their next lift.

When Urquhart was informed about this decision, he expressed his concern to the British Lieutenant General Browning, commander of the British Airborne Corps and deputy to the American commander of the 1st Allied Airborne Army. Urquhart was told that the whole operation was to be 'bottom to top' (from 'south' to 'north'), which meant that the 101st and the 82nd US Airborne Divisions would be taken across in two airlifts while the 1st British Airborne Division would be carried in three lifts. Browning added: 'To your south everything has to go well. If not, there is a fair chance of getting slaughtered.'[10] This meant that the British airborne forces, which faced 'the toughest task in the most advanced position' were allocated three lifts.[11]

The 1st British Airborne Division consisted of three brigades, the 1st and 4th Parachute Brigade and the 1st Airlanding Brigade. The 1st Independent Polish Parachute Brigade supplemented the division. The first lift included the 1st, 2nd and 3rd Parachute Battalion of the 1st Parachute Brigade and most of the three Airlanding Battalions of the 1st Airlanding Brigade. Two batteries of the Light Regiment, one anti-tank battery (Royal Artillery), a detachment sappers (Royal Engineers), the Reconnaissance Squadron and two medical units also came in on the first lift.

According to the plan the 4th Parachute Brigade would be flown in on the second lift on the next day (18 September) and was to be dropped on Ginkel Heath near Ede. The third lift was to carry the 1st Independent Polish Parachute Brigade. Originally this brigade was to land near Elden on 19 September, but due to the fact that this area south of Arnhem was by then occupied by the Germans, the Polish paratroopers were dropped near Driel.

The 52nd (Lowland) Infantry Division was kept in reserve in England and was to be taken across after the capture of Deelen airfield.

This schedule implicated that both landing and dropping zones had to be defended until the arrival of the second and third lift. The safeguarding of these areas for the second lift was assigned to the 1st Airlanding Brigade as a whole. Only a single battalion of this brigade was available to protect the arrival of the third lift.

One of the units, part of the 1st Airlanding Brigade, was the 7th (Galloway) Battalion The King's Own Scottish Borderers (7 KOSB). This battalion was assigned DZ-Y at Ginkel Heath near Ede. It was to occupy and hold the ground until the arrival of the 4th Parachute Brigade on D + 1. The Pathfinders of No. 3 Platoon 21st Independent Parachute Company were to take care of the markings on the ground.

All these arrangements implicated that on the first day of the operation to take the road bridge across the Rhine at Arnhem Major General Urquhart could only count on one of his three brigades, i.e. the 1st Parachute Brigade. This also meant that at the most important area of Operation Market Garden the smallest number of paratroopers was deployed. The transport of the division in three separate lifts was one of the biggest mistakes that was made during the planning stages and of which Major General Urquhart would later say that 'this handicap was never overcome'.[12]

Cap badge The King's Own Scottish Borderers.

(PHOTO: COURTESY R.N. SIGMOND)

With hindsight it would have been better to have chosen other drop and landing zones for the second and third lifts. That would have meant that the units guarding the ground could have participated in the attack on the road bridge on the very first day. Assigning the task to cover these zones to the 1st Airlanding Brigade only added to the difficulties of carrying the division in three separate airlifts.

As a result Urquhart's division was severely under strength and was unable to reach the road bridge quickly enough to establish a secure bridgehead.

Despite some ground fog, Sunday 17 September was a beautiful day with excellent visibility. The losses underway were negligible. Some gliders had to crash-land in England after their tow ropes had broken, some others crashed in the North Sea and as there was no serious flak only a few went down over Holland.

At 12.40 hours the Pathfinders of the 21st Independent Parachute Company reached their DZ north of Heelsum. Their landing went smoothly and they started with their task without any serious problems. Half an hour later they had laid out the large white nylon panels and put the transmitting beacons and smoke canisters in position on the DZs, which not only indicated the RVs or rendezvous points but also the wind direction. Whilst preparing all the necessary markings they also took fifteen prisoners of war and 'captured' a German staff car.

A few minutes later they heard the throbbing engines of the approaching planes.

After the Pathfinders, the first lift arrived. At approximately 13.00 hours the airborne troops reached their LZs and DZs. The first batch consisted of one hundred and thirty tugs towing a glider each and carrying the 1st Airlanding Brigade to LZ-S to the north and one hundred and fifty gliders carrying one anti-tank battery, two batteries of the Light Regiment, jeeps, motorcycles and Bren carriers to LZ-Z to the west of Wolfheze. Three quarters of an hour later paratroopers of the 1st Parachute Brigade jumped from 143 transport planes of the USAF above DZ-X north of Heelsum. Everything went according to plan and Major J.A. Hibbert noted in his diary that 'the Air Force gave us a perfect flight in'.[13]

It later turned out to be the most successful airborne landing of the whole war.

Of course there were some accidents. The undercarriage of a few gliders collapsed and after a rough landing some jeeps were heavily damaged and put out of action. One glider landed in the middle of some trees. Some Hamilcars dug their nose wheels into the loose soil and came to an abrupt halt with their long, light tail rising into the air. Some gliders landed upside down. A few collided on the ground and some others crashed into the trees.

Of the 320 gliders that left England 283 (88.4 percent) landed on or close to their LZs. Eleven men – mostly glider pilots - were killed outright or died as a result of these landing accidents.[14] Not a single plane was lost during this lift.

At approximately 15.30 hours three battalions of the 1st Parachute Brigade left in the direction of Arnhem. The 1st Battalion moved forward to the Amsterdamseweg through Wolfheze, the 2nd Battalion took the Benedendorpsweg in Oosterbeek and the 3rd advanced on Arnhem through Kievitsdel and the Utrechtseweg (see map no. 2).

The initial hours of the operation had gone well and the airborne troops did not meet any serious opposition, but shortly afterwards the first problems began. These were mainly caused by the distance to be covered between the DZs and LZs and the actual target of the whole operation.

The plan for the Market part of the attack stipulated that both DZs and LZs would be within a range of six to nine miles from the Arnhem road bridge.

General James Gavin, commanding the 82nd US Airborne Division, would later say: 'I could not believe my ears. This was against all we had learned both in theory and practice.' The element of surprise, which is so important for a successful airborne operation, would have gone by the time the British reached the road bridge. The success of any airborne landing depends on what happens during the first twenty-four hours and according to General Gavin the airborne troops should have been dropped on top of their targets. He further said: 'I have great worries about the whole battle plan of the 1st British Airborne Division. On paper it looked more like an exercise than a real operation.'[15]

The time the British would need to reach Arnhem signified a double risk. Because the vital element of surprise was lost one would have to accept the possibility that the Germans would put up fierce resistance and try to block the roads to the centre of Arnhem and reinforce the defence of the road bridge.

The selection of DZs and LZs to the west of Arnhem became necessary when the RAF refused to execute the landings near the Arnhem road bridge because of high density flak. It later appeared that there were only a few anti-aircraft guns positioned in the vicinity of the bridge.

Moreover, the planners found the pastureland south of Arnhem not suitable for the landing of gliders. Malburgen polder is bisected by wide ditches and lies below sea level. Therefore they came to the conclusion that the ground was too soggy. However, it is remarkable that during the preparations for Operation Comet, the sixteenth plan that was cancelled prior to Market Garden, this terrain was considered suitable. The polder was even included as DZ for the third day of Market Garden. The fact that in the end the Polish Brigade did not land in that area has an entirely different reason.

At half past seven on the evening of 17 September a Dutch police officer noticed that the bridge across the Rhine was completely deserted. The usual number of German sentries, which ranged between twenty and thirty men and who operated some small anti-aircraft guns, had fled in the afternoon when the first airborne troops landed. If the Allies had dropped a *coup-de-main* force on the south side of the bridge they could have taken it without any resistance. The first paratroopers only arrived at the northern ramp at 20.00 hours that night and shortly before a SS unit had taken up defensive positions on the south side.[16]

In his *Memoirs* Montgomery admitted to have made a big tactical mistake and that he assumed full responsibility. He wrote: 'I should have ordered the Second Army and the 1st Allied Airborne Army to drop at least one parachute brigade as close as possible to the bridge in order to take it within a couple of minutes. In that case strong defensive positions could have been taken up. However, I failed to do so.'[17]

At approximately 10.00 hours the battalion took off from the Down Ampney and Blakehill Farm airfields in the southeast of England for what was to be its first and only action of the war. In his war diary the commanding officer, Lieutenant Colonel Payton Reid mentions that the battalion departed in light and low cloud. This forced some gliders to disconnect their towropes over England and make a premature landing. Over the North Sea the skies were clear. Here another three gliders went down, but the Air Sea Rescue Service saved their crews and airborne troops within fifteen minutes.

Lieutenant Colonel R. Payton Reid, commanding officer 7th Battalion The King's Own Scottish Borderers.

(PHOTO: COURTESY R.N. SIGMOND)

Upon reaching the Dutch coast one could see the inundated islands of the province of Zeeland with only a few buildings sticking out of the water.[18] Over Schouwen-Duiveland a glider got into trouble, but the pilot managed to put it safely on the ground. On the way there was no mention of any flak.

At approximately two miles from their landing zone the towropes were disconnected and the gliders started their approach. At 13.30 hours the battalion landed in forty-six Horsas on LZ-S near Reyerskamp Farm.

Upon landing two gliders crashed into the trees at the edge of the LZ, which regrettably caused the death of one glider pilot. There was also a lot of material damage. Because of the soft ground many gliders had their undercarriage crash through the bottom of the fuselage, which blocked the unloading of some motorcycles and an anti-tank gun.

Of the initial fifty-six gliders ten did not arrive at all. This implicated that on the first day of the operation two platoons could not be deployed and that three mortar platoons, three machine-gun sections, and two detachments of anti-tanks gunners were missing. Part of the men and material were flown in on the second and the third lift.[19]

On the ground the airborne forces were welcomed by the Regimental march *Blue Bonnets over the Border*, piped by Willie Ford from Selkirk. He played his bagpipes at the RV until every man had reported at the assembly point. Forty officers and seven hundred other ranks had arrived safely.

At 14.00 hours that same day 350 guns from the British Second Army opened up, which meant the start of Operation Garden. Half an hour later Lieutenant General Sir Brian 'Hurricane' Horrocks and his XXX Corps started the advance from Neerpelt in northern Belgium towards the road bridge at Arnhem.

THE GERMAN DEFENCE

So far the crossing to Holland and the actual allied landings had not encountered significant problems, but almost immediately thereafter the general situation for the British airborne forces changed dramatically. During their advance towards Arnhem the battalions, that had landed near Wolfheze and Heelsum, met with fierce German resistance.

The Germans realized that Arnhem was of vital strategic importance. If the Allies should manage to establish a bridgehead across the Rhine, they could bypass the Siegfried Line and the road to the Ruhr area and the North German Plain would lie open. At the same time an allied push to the IJsselmeer would isolate the Germans in the west of Holland from their *Heimat*. A swift and well-organised counterattack was required to safe the day.

Luck came to the rescue of the Germans. The accidental presence of the *II SS Panzer Korps* (Armoured Corps) under the command of SS General Wilhelm Bittrich, just to the east and north of the British operation area and consisting of the decimated *9.* and *10. SS Panzer Division* enabled the Germans to react very quickly. Right from the start the striking power of these forces was to have a decisive influence on the outcome of the battle.

Major General Urquhart, who during the briefing by Lieutenant General Browning was informed that the Germans in the Arnhem area could only deploy a single brigade and a couple of tanks, came to face an enemy of superior strength both in numbers and armament.[20]

After its retreat from France on 8 September and two days before Eisenhower's decision to go ahead with Operation Market Garden, the *II SS Panzer Korps* was given marching orders to an area to the north and northeast of Arnhem. The idea was that one of its divisions was to be brought back to full strength, while the other was to proceed to Siegen in Germany to be reinforced.

During the week preceding the start of Operation Market Garden the *Panzer Korps* had reached its holding position north of Arnhem and in the Achterhoek, but was hardly up to regimental strength. However, it was equipped with armoured cars, tanks, self-propelled guns and mortars. After 17 September any necessary ordnance that was lacking was quickly brought to the front from Germany.

The presence of both German armoured divisions to the north and east of Arnhem was already known to the Allied Supreme Command. In his report to the combined operational Chiefs of Staff in Europe Eisenhower had written that their presence was confirmed by his intelligence staff.[21] Between 1 and 17 September a steady flow of reports from, amongst others, the Dutch resistance had reached the various headquarters.

On 7 September it was understood from *Ultra* -the allied code-name for all intelligence gathered from decoded German radio signals – that the remains of the *II SS Panzer Korps* had reached Holland. A week later this message was confirmed by the Dutch resistance group Albrecht with the additional information that the corps was somewhere in the vicinity of Arnhem.

The allied commanders had detailed information at their disposal but Montgomery, who had already been informed on 10 September, chose to ignore these intelligence reports.

The head of the intelligence staff of the 1st British Airborne Division, Major Brian Urquhart, consequently warned Lieutenant General Browning on several occasions but without success. However, this officer was so worried that he ordered the RAF to take aerial photographs. On 15 September he was able to produce pictures that clearly showed the presence of modern Mark III and Mark IV tanks, self-propelled guns and armoured vehicles. Browning ignored Brian Urquhart's warnings and said that the German armour was not operational and was most probably made of cardboard. The major could not convince his superior officer of the value of this hard evidence. Montgomery's plan had been declared sacrosanct and the major was sent on sick leave on account of 'nervous strain and exhaustion'. He would later say that 'nothing was to disturb the illusion that the operation was going to be a success'.[22]

While the British did nothing, Eisenhower did. The intelligence report from his headquarters dated 16 September is very clear and straightforward: 'The 9th SS Panzer Division, and presumably the 10th, has been reported withdrawing to the Arnhem area in Holland; there they will probably collect new tanks from a depot reported in the area of Cleves'.[23]

Eisenhower sent his Chief of Staff Bedell Smith to the self-willed Montgomery but, just as the warnings of all the other 'messengers of doom', the latter also ignored this one. A proposal to change the original plan was also rejected. Both Browning and Montgomery doubted whether both German armoured divisions were operational and the latter was more worried about the ground conditions of the landing areas.[24]

The operation was to go on at all cost. Despite the fact that

Eisenhower, Montgomery and Brereton were fully aware of the actual situation the units of the First Allied Airborne Army were not officially informed about the presence of the German armoured divisions.

Although Eisenhower could have intervened, he did not undertake any action. His already strained relationship with Montgomery would have worsened when the supreme commander should have cancelled the operation and it would have appeared that he doubted Montgomery's capacity as a field commander. Besides, he did not want to enter into the Field Marshal's competency. This would have been highly unusual. Moreover, Montgomery was the best judge of the actual situation.[25]

Practically from the moment of the landings Urquhart's airborne troops found themselves under adverse circumstances that could not be adjusted. They did not have any tanks, armoured vehicles or heavy artillery.

Lady Luck had even more in store for the Germans. At the moment of the landings a SS unit was having a field exercise within walking distance of the LZs. The SS *Panzer Grenadier Ausbildungs- und Ersatz Bataillon 16* (Trainings and Reserve Battalion) under the command of Major Krafft was partly based in Oosterbeek while the remainder was billeted at Arnhem. On the morning of 17 September the 2. *Kompanie* of this battalion happened to be on a training exercise in the woods near Wolfheze. At the moment of the landings the company was at the Hotel Wolfheze, where Krafft established his headquarters and ordered the 2. and 4. *Kompanie* to take up defensive positions along the Wolfhezerweg where they were to stop the advancing British battalions west of Arnhem. One and a half hours after the first landings and just before the British set out towards Arnhem both companies had taken up their positions along the Wolfhezerweg stretching from the Utrechtseweg near De Bilderberg Hotel to an area north of Wolfheze railway station. In doing so they practically blocked both northern routes of the airborne troops to the road bridge. Krafft anticipated that the British would only advance along the Utrechtseweg and the Utrecht-Arnhem railway line and would not use the former Ede-Arnhem trunk road or the Benedendorpsweg along the Rhine.[26] However, his judgement failed him and in the evening of 17 September the 2nd Parachute Battalion of the 1st Parachute Brigade managed to reach the Arnhem bridge via this last mentioned approach road (see map no. 2).

After the initial panic had faded Field Marshal Model, commander of the Army Group B, started organizing the German defence. The *9. SS Panzer Division (Hohenstaufen)* together with some other units were directed to the Arnhem bridge to block the approaches to the town centre.

The division was also ordered to execute reconnaissance patrols in the direction of Nijmegen and put up defensive positions in Arnhem. Shortly afterwards the line Mariëndaal-Kema-Brink-railway line-Oosterbeek station-Dreijenseweg was manned. At 21.30 hours its command post was established at Mariëndaal and self-propelled guns and field artillery were brought into position.

The heart of the German defence was situated south of the bridges across the river Waal near Nijmegen with defensive positions north of the city near Bemmel and Elst. This decision was taken to prevent the British Second Army of linking up with the airborne forces near Arnhem. Urquhart's division was to be completely cut off and for that purpose the *10. SS Panzer Division (Frundsberg)* was ordered to take up positions in the Betuwe area. However, the Germans arrived too late at the bridge at Arnhem. In the meantime the 2nd Parachute Battalion under the command of Lieutenant Colonel Frost had lodged itself on the northern ramp and the German *Panzer Division* had to make a detour. This proved even more difficult when it appeared that earlier that morning the ferry at Huissen had been hit and sunk. In the end the division used the ferry at Pannerden and from there it moved on to Nijmegen by way of Bemmel.

A few hours after the first airborne landings the Germans had built two strong defensive lines at all access roads to Arnhem. The first practically blocked both the Ede and Heelsum roads and the second in the western part of the town blocked the route to the bridge. The light armament of the British made it impossible for them to break through the German line around the inner city. While the situation for the German defenders improved by the hour, the 2nd Parachute Battalion on the bridge waited in vain for reinforcements.

During the night of the 17th and early morning of the 18th the first trains carrying tanks from a Trainings and Reserve Battalion in Germany started moving in the direction of Arnhem.

Within a short time the Germans succeeded in supplementing the troops in and around Arnhem with army, air force and coastal defence units. The fighting strength of many of these units, with the exception of SS units, was not particularly great. However, this was partly compensated by the flexible German military organization, which enabled them to react quickly and adequately in emergency situations.[27]

According to some sources the quick German response was also made possible because, after an American glider was shot down near Vught, the Germans found a full set of notes describing the operational plan on the body of an officer inside the plane.[28] Unfortunately the glider went down near the headquarters of the German General Student who, with his 1. *Fallschirm Armee*, (Parachute Army) was defending the Brabant positions. Within a couple of hours the plan was on Student's desk and the Germans were in possession of a rough outline of the '*Einsatzbefehle, Stärke, Gliederung und Absicht der Luftlandeoperation*' (order of battle, battle strength, communications and further operational details).[29]

Major General Urquhart also thought that the Germans had used these documents to get an insight into the marching orders, strength and composition of the deployed allied forces and the purpose of the operation. In his book entitled *Arnhem* the commanding officer of the 1st British Airborne Division wrote: 'The nonchalance or deliberate disobedience of one officer has compensated the Germans for the element of surprise of our unexpected attack.'[30]

However, it is very doubtful to what extent the Germans made use of this information. After the war the American writer Cornelius Ryan had an interview with General Bittrich, commanding officer of *II* SS *Panzer Korps*. In this interview the latter confirmed never to have seen these documents. According to Ryan Field Marshal Model did not find these papers of any value and for that reason did not pass them on to either Bittrich or General Field Marshal Von Rundstedt, the German supreme commander in Western Europe.

A statement from *Obersturmbannführer* Harzer, commanding the 9. SS *Panzer Division* who did see these documents, also confirmed the little value the Germans attached to this information. In an interview with Ryan he claimed that the operational orders were of little use. Only the details referring to the landings were accurate. However, the Germans distrusted the captured plans and had serious doubts about their authenticity.[31]

It is certain that the possession of these papers did not contribute to the quick German response. If Bittrich should have had any knowledge of these documents, it would not have made him change his plans and both Model and Harzer were aware of their contents, but did not make any use of them.

Moreover, it is far from certain whether the Germans got hold of the complete plans of Operation Market Garden. General Student thought he had. However, copies of these documents were only handed over to staff officers. According to Student the shot down plane was a Waco glider. In his book entitled *A Bridge Too Far* Ryan writes that part of Browning's headquarters was flown over in Wacos and that one of these went down near Vught.

Whether this plane carried a staff officer with notes of the operational plan or just an officer with an order of the day for the 101st US Airborne Division is unknown.

It is still not certain which documents were in Student's possession. From the appearance of a number of Messerschmitts over the DZs and LZs at the exact moment on which the aircraft of the second lift should have arrived on Monday, 18 September, it can be concluded that the Germans were aware of the full operational plan and that in circles of the German *Luftwaffe* one did believe in the contents of the found documents based on which the necessary countermeasures were taken. Model's headquarters also warned all anti-aircraft batteries.[32]

The Germans also started to strengthen their defences more to the west of Arnhem. Rauter, Commander-in-Chief of the SS as well as Chief of the German Police in Holland, issued an order that an eventual advance of allied airborne forces in western direction was to be stopped by all available army units.

General Von Tettau quickly established his headquarters in a villa on Grebbeberg from where he formed the so-called *Westgruppe*, which is wrongly denoted as *Division Von Tettau*.

This division was no regular unit, but a motley collection of all sorts of units that were hastely scraped together from the west and centre of Holland. Von Tettau had been a staff officer at General Christiansen's German Armed Forces Command in The Netherlands. He was a kind of inspector in charge of military training and also commanded several units that were stationed along the Waal river. Earlier in the war he had been a divisional commander on the Russian front.

The *Westgruppe* was ordered to attack and close off the DZs and LZs from the west.

The first unit to be called up was the SS *Wach-Bataillon 3* (most Dutch SS), which was on guard duty at the Amersfoort concentration camp. In the afternoon of 17 September Rauter phoned 2nd Lieutenant Naumann, aide-de-camp of the Austrian commanding officer Major Helle, and told him that the major and his staff were to report to Von Tettau on Grebbeberg as soon as possible. This battalion consisted for a small part of young men recruited from candidates for the *Arbeitseinsatz* i.e. forced labour in Germany and for the larger part of deranged Dutchmen who were press-ganged from a camp for criminal delinquents, from Borstal homes and from various prisons.[33] All of them had signed a German contract and were drafted into the Dutch SS.

Also incorporated in this battalion were ethnic Germans. They had the German nationality and lived outside the German national borders of 1937 and Austria. During the occupation of Holland these ethnic Germans living there were drafted into the German army.[34]

The high ranking officers of the SS *Wach-Bataillon 3* were all Germans, while some of the NCOs were Dutch. The Dutch 1st Lieutenant Bronkhorst led the *1. Kompanie*, but all other companies had German officers. Besides the *1. Kompanie*, the *3.* under Hink, the *4.* under Bartsch, the *5.* under Kühne and the *6.* under Fernau were all on duty in Amersfoort on the day of the allied airborne landings while the *2. Kompanie* under commanding officer Ziegler was on the way to Germany with a group of prisoners. The SS *Wach-Bataillon 3* consisted in total of about seven to eight hundred men.

In the course of Sunday General Christiansen arranged a further supplementation of the Division Von Tettau. Besides the SS *Wach-Bataillon 3* the *Westgruppe* that evening consisted of the *10. Schiffs-Stamm-Abteilung* (hastily assembled troops from the Belgian and French coastal defences), detachments from the SS NCO School 'Arnheim' under the command of Lieutenant Colonel Lippert and a *Fliegerhorst Bataillon*, a converted air force infantry battalion composed of ground crews from Soesterberg airfield and some abandoned airfields in Germany. The SS *Ausbildungs Bataillon* under Major Eberwein was already on the march to Rhenen.

Furthermore, Von Tettau had some units at his disposal that were in the direct vicinity of the landing areas viz. the *6. Kompanie* of the *14. Schiffs-Stamm-Abteilung* from Opheusden, which had crossed the Rhine east of Grebbeberg and was dispatched in the direction of Arnhem through Wageningen and one battery of the *Artillerie Regiment 184* from Bennekom. As not enough guns were available this detachment was deployed as an infantry unit and was to hold the woods to the east of the village.[35]

Initially the *Bataillon Krafft*, which had moved into positions along the Wolfhezerweg, was also under the command of Von Tettau. In the night of the 17th and early morning of the 18th the companies of this *Bataillon* pulled back towards Schaarsbergen. As a result Krafft entered the defensive lines of the 9. SS *Panzer Division* and was therefore withdrawn from the *Westgruppe*.

Both SS units from the *Westgruppe* were well trained, but the battle strength of the *Schiffs-Stamm-Abteilungen* was 'next to nothing'. These 'sailors' had no idea of how to fight an infantry battle. The same applied to the *Fliegerhorst Bataillon*, 'a rather grand title for troops that never had any training other than to roll barrels of petrol'.[36]

In general the SS units were made up of very young soldiers whereas the other detachments included mostly elderly men that were not suited to serve in the frontline. According to Von Tettau their battle strength, measured by training and armament, was mediocre. With the exception of their counterparts in the SS units most officers had had little or no military training, let alone any battle experience. However, their commanding general concluded that 'the successes and continuous encouragement made that their pleasure to take part in the battle increased by the hour'.

Von Tettau assessed the actual situation and like a great strategist came to the conclusion that 'only extensive and comprehensive countermeasures could thwart the plans of the enemy'.[37]

The strategy he devised was extremely simple and consisted of a twofold attack on the LZs and DZs. One was to be executed from Wageningen and the other from Ede from the north. This would split the area that the British were holding in two.

Part of the available German forces in Wageningen was deployed against the airborne troops near Renkum and Heelsum. Lippert and his SS NCO School detachment were ordered to move straight to Renkum and were to be flanked by the *10. Schiffs-Stamm-Abteilung* on the right and by the *Fliegerhorst Bataillon* on the left.

They were to join the *6./14. Schiffs-Stamm-Abteilung* in its front position east of Wageningen and that of the 184th Artillery Regiment in Bennekom.

During the *Westgruppe's* push from the north an important role was played by the *Wach-Bataillon* from Amersfoort. It was directed to Ede to clear the woods east of this town and Ginkel Heath.

Shortly after consulting Von Tettau the reconnaissance unit of the *Wach-Bataillon* in Amersfoort was instructed by telephone from Grebbeberg headquarters to leave immediately for Ede via Woudenberg and Scherpenzeel. The other companies and the artillery were also directed to Ede to engage the British as quickly as possible. A few minutes later Helle and his adjutant drove to Ede to establish their headquarters in Hotel-Pension De Langenberg.

That evening would see the first skirmishes with the British who were guarding the DZs and LZs. The German forces that were stationed in the direct vicinity of Ede and the SS *Wach-Bataillon* were on the verge of engaging the 7th Battalion The King's Own Scottish Borderers on and around Ginkel Heath.

THE POSITIONS OF 7 KOSB AT GINKEL HEATH

Around 15.00 hours, almost one and a half hours after landing near Wolfheze, the 7th Battalion KOSB left its LZ and moved in the direction of Ede. En route it did not meet any significant resistance and it captured some German soldiers. The Germans had apparently been so surprised by the landings that the British even caught some Germans unawares when cutting firewood.[38]

A Company 7 KOSB was the first to leave and was assigned to close off the Ede-Arnhem road between Zuid Ginkel Café and Planken Wambuis Café. No. 4 Platoon took up positions at the edge of the wood east of Zuid Ginkel Café on both sides of the road and company headquarters were established in Planken Wambuis Café. (see map no. 3).

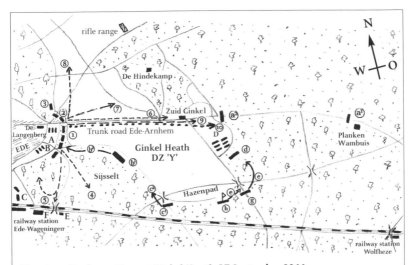

Map 3:   Battle positions at Ginkel Heath 17 September 1944.

A = Simon Stevin barracks
B = Elias Beeckman barracks
C = Maurits- en Johan Willem
     Friso barracks
D = Work camp Het Wijde Veld
E = Signal box 19A
F = ENKA rayon works

**British battle positions and patrols 7th
Battalion KOSB**

a¹ = headquarters A company
a² = no. 4 platoon A company
b¹ = battle position B company
b² = patrol B company
c¹ = battle position C company
c² = patrol C company
d = battle position D company
e = patrols
g = battle position Staff Company
h = headquarters 7 KOSB

German battle positions and patrols
  1 = battle positions 7.Stammkompanie
       4. SS-Ausbildungs-Ersatz Bataillon
  2 = 2 sections 7.Stammkompanie
  3 = 2 companies of a Kraft-
       fahrersatzabteilung.
  4 = Stammkompanie 20.Schiffs-Stamm-
       Abteilung
  5 = 2 Wehrmacht artillery batteries
  6 = 1 section 7.Stammkompanie
7 and 8 = 2 reconnaissance patrols
       7.Stammkompanie
  9 = Jagdkompanie SS Wach Bataillon 3
  10 = 4.Kompanie SS Wach Bataillon 3

The Planken Wambuis Café on Amsterdamseweg at Ede. A Coy Headquarters, 7 KOSB during the Battle for Ginkel Heath.

(PHOTO: ARCHIVES SOCIETY 'OLD EDE', NO. 313248)

Ginkel Heath is a rather flat and completely open terrain with to the west and south the long drawn out woods called De Sijsselt, to the east the woods of Ginkelse Zand and to the north the Ede-Arnhem road. According to plan the other companies of 7 KOSB were direct-ed to their positions round the heath at about 16.00 hours. Half an hour later B and C Companies reached the woods on the northern edge of De Sijsselt and took up positions along the west and south side of Ginkel Heath. Soon the British discovered that they found themselves on a military practice ground of the Germans. Appa-rently the intelligence reports were correct. They had confirmed that Ginkel Heath, east of Ede, was used by the German army and was roughly similar to the training ground of the British army near their base in Aldershot.[39]

B Company dug in and was grateful to use the 'very excellent' trenches that had been left by the Germans. This company was posi-tioned nearest to the Simon Stevin barracks and approximately only one mile lay between them and the German garrison in Ede. An anti-tank gun was put in position within range of the Ede-

Arnhem road, which was about seven hundred yards away. Furthermore, the men positioned some machine-guns and two 3-inch mortars. To avoid detection the order was issued to only fire during darkness in case of emergency.

Battalion headquarters and D Company, which was kept in reserve, were both located in the woods south of the fly-over on the 'Hazenpad' (rabbit run), which was the popular nickname of the current motorway A12 between Utrecht and Oberhausen in Germany. This road was under construction at the time of the landings and was so called by the Dutch to indicate that the Germans could use this road to flee to their *Heimat*.

That evening, in order to prevent the Germans from firing at the DZ, a platoon of D Company was ordered to occupy the sheds of the work camp 't Wijde Veld, which at that moment was situated east of the bicycle track near the sheep fold.[40]

When the airborne soldiers approached the camp they saw through their binoculars men digging trenches. However, they did not seem to be soldiers. Upon entering the sheds they were enthusiastically welcomed by the inhabitants, hands were shaken and children gathered around the airborne troops. It turned out that the camp housed seventy evacuees from Stavenisse in the province of Zeeland. On 6 March 1944 they had been forced by the Germans to leave their homes and were taken to Ginkel Heath in coaches and by train. Daily life in the camp was as in a 'normal village'. The men worked on the surrounding farms and the children went to 'school' in the canteen.

The British requested to speak to the leader of the camp, but neither he nor anybody else spoke English. One of the Borderers tried to communicate in Yiddish, but this also did not work. The man was taken to battalion headquarters and was interrogated by a lieutenant who spoke fluent German. The commanding officer decided to have the man brought back to the camp and ordered the inhabitants not to leave the sheds. The airborne soldiers promised to protect them as best as they could and searched the camp for any

Work camp 't Wijde Veld on Ginkel Heath.

Germans. After the all clear the platoon established its headquarters in one of the trenches dug by the civilians.[41]

So far the British had not sighted any Germans and D Company was also ordered to avoid engaging the enemy at all costs.[42] In the afternoon all positions to protect DZ-Y had been taken up and all companies of 7 KOSB were entrenched in the woods surrounding Ginkel Heath.

At about 19.00 hours that evening the first patrols were sent out to gather information on the enemy positions. After having captured some prisoners of war the British learned about the presence of approximately six hundred Germans in the two Ede barracks nearest to Ginkel Heath and that reinforcements were on the move north of Ede.[43]

However, right from the beginning of the landings no proper communications were possible between the various British companies. As during the whole Battle of Arnhem the divisional signals system was totally inadequate and in the wooded area round Ginkel Heath the available wireless sets were completely useless.[44]

The only news 7 KOSB received by radio was the report on the landings near Arnhem broadcasted the next morning on the BBCs Nine O'Clock News.

Because of the great distance and ruptures in the lines normal telephone contact was also next to impossible. The only means of communications between the various British units, both during the day and the night, was through patrols and runners. Even battalion headquarters could not establish radio contact with the other units.

All this made the overall situation for the various companies rather awkward. It also appeared that the heath was too wide to be properly defended, which meant that the northwestern edge nearest to Ede was almost unprotected.[45]

7 KOSB now found itself under very adverse circumstances and could not count on any divisional support. Radio contact with divisional headquarters was not possible and the battalion was now separated from all other battalions by thick woodland and quite some distance. 7 KOSB was completely on its own.

Upon nightfall men of the Advance Party of the 4th Parachute Brigade managed to reach battalion headquarters. They had landed on the first lift to mark the RVs of their brigade with green and blue smoke canisters shortly before next morning the landing of the brigade should take place.[46]

In the meantime the allied landings had not gone unnoticed to the citizens of Ede. Many of them had witnessed the landing of the paratroopers from a distance out of their skylights. Not much later they had heard that British troops had been seen in the vicinity of Ginkel Heath.

Both civilians and German forces thought that the British would move westwards and that the liberation of Ede was at hand. It was rumoured that the airborne troops had already reached Simon Stevin barracks and the citizens of Ede rejoiced in the expectation that the German occupation would be over in a couple of hours. The wildest rumours were going around. No one realized that the British were waiting for the second lift after which they were to move to the east.

After the appearance of the first British forces at the edges of Ginkel Heath the Germans at Simon Stevin barracks were put on the highest alert. They not only feared the airborne troops, but also possible actions by the Dutch resistance. On the previous night the local German commanding officer Labahn had ordered the summary execution of two young Dutch boys, Ab Meijler from Goes and Adri Verkerk from Amersfoort, who had been arrested by Dutch members of the German police and were shot in the bushes opposite the barracks.[47]

While the above mentioned *Ortskommandant* was still busy assessing the damage done by the bombardment of the Enka works and was supervising the fire-fighting operations, his second in command ordered the *7. Stammkompanie* to take up positions to the east of Simon Stevin barracks. This was the first unit that engaged the airborne troops (see map no.3).[48]

After his return from the Enka works to Simon Stevin barracks the *Ortskommandant* ordered all available forces in the Ede area to report as soon as possible. This had little result as only some small units did report, which moreover appeared to be not really '*kampfbereit*' (prepared for battle).

Besides, the troops that were already present in these barracks could not be described as an elite force. The *7. Stammkompanie* consisted of recruits and reserves of the *4. SS Panzer Grenadier Ausbildungs- und Ersatz Bataillon*. They were declared unfit for field service and served their country by guarding military depots. Also present was a detachment of *Luftwaffe* personnel.

The commanding officer of the barracks did not think very highly of the troops at his disposal. In his report on the events of 17 and 18 September Labahn wrote rather belittling that many of the reserves had a cultural and civil service background and that a number of them was still wearing civvies on the 17th. He further wrote that 'the reserves, who had arrived a short while earlier, had to change into uniforms when already at their battle positions.' In

Simon Stevin barracks in Ede, situated on the western edge of Ginkel Heath. The foundations were laid by the Dutch before WW II. The Germans later built the barracks during the war. During the Battle of Arnhem *7. Kompanie* of *4. SS Panzer Grenadier Ausbildungs- und Ersatz Bataillon* and a detachment of the *Luftwaffe* were billeted here.

(PHOTO: ARCHIVES SOCIETY 'OLD EDE', NO. 311163)

the same report he gave the following striking example of their fighting power: 'The SS NCOs had to instruct their troops how to load their rifles and how to secure and use their hand-grenades.' Labahn could only describe them as '*nur Waschlappen*' (face flannels).[49]

Small wonder that on the 'front' things did not go as they should.

The Germans took into account that the British planned to take Ede and push on in a westerly direction. Moreover, at that moment they did not know where the British were and they did not have any information on the strength and armament of the airborne forces. For those reasons the *Ortskommandant* had reinforced the positions round the barracks and had send out some patrols. The German *7. Kompanie* was ordered to extend the German positions south of the Arnhem road and east of Simon Stevin barracks by bending away to the south and southwest as far as the adjoining woods. Two sections were positioned north of the trunk road. One

Maurits barracks near Ede-Wageningen railway station. In September 1944 *20. Schiffs-Stamm-Abteilung* was billeted here.

company of the *20. Schiffs-Stamm-Abteilung* from the Maurits and Johan Willem Friso barracks in Ede was deployed on the right flank of the *7. Kompanie* and was directed to the south straight across De Sijsselt woods.[50] Two *Wehrmacht* artillery batteries from Wageningen were ordered to move to the right of the *20. Schiffs-Stamm-Abteilung* at the first level crossing of the Ede to Arnhem railway line near signal box 19A. Their right flank was to bear off to the north.

These final orders were apparently not executed very '*pünktlich*' (to the letter), as the *Ortskommandant* did not mention any positive result in his *Gefechtsbericht* (war diary). Most likely none of these units got very far in the woods of De Sijsselt and were only able to form a defensive cordon to the east of Simon Stevin and Beeckman barracks where they took up positions on the higher wooded ground at the edge of Ginkel Heath.

To the left of both sections of the *7. Kompanie* and north of the Ede-Arnhem road two substandard companies of a *Kraftfahrersatzabteilung*, a supplementary detachment of lorry drivers was deployed. In the early hours of the evening both these companies were ordered to abandon their positions and to return to their lorries. Next a section of the *7. Kompanie* was ordered to take up these positions and to extend the defensive line to the rifle range in a northerly direction.

At the same time two patrols were directed to the north and northeast. One section of the 7. *Kompanie* managed to reach the woods west of the Zuid Ginkel Café via the north end of the trunk road and was added to a company of the SS *Wach Bataillon 3* from Amersfoort. Altogether it was an attempt to arrange a 'provisional protection of Ede'.

However, the majority of the *Luftwaffe* personnel together with some corporals and men of the *Waffen-SS* did not believe in this '*vorläufige Sicherung von Ede*' (provisional protection of Ede) and tried to leave their positions on their own. Some SS NCOs succeeded in ordering these 'retreating' men back to their front line positions. When the *Ortskommandant* was informed about these events he even considered the summary execution of 'all these cowards' as a deterrent. In the end he decided against this measure because otherwise he would have had to execute at least every fifth man ('*mindestens jeden fünften Mann hätte standrechtlich verurteilen müssen*'). He could not afford to do that as the forces at his disposal were already minimal. He was even forced to compose a small unit that was ordered to take each escapee, regardless of rank, back to the front line.[51]

The German reconnaissance patrols, which were directed to the north and northeast, reported that they had not observed any enemy forces, but had had 'some fire contact with the enemy' in the northeastern area.

Shortly afterwards a first engagement took also place near Planken Wambuis Café. Suddenly a German ambulance and a small squad car en route to Arnhem passed by the British headquarters of A Company and were shot at. When the door of the ambulance was opened it turned out to be full of heavily armed Germans, which were immediately taken prisoner. For the rest of the day all remained quiet near the café and this was the only action A Company was involved in that Sunday.[52]

Remains of German trenches, manholes, machine gun and mortar positions at the edge of the woods east of Ede. (see map nos. 3 and 4)

(PHOTOS: AUTHOR)

Late that afternoon Helle, in command of the *Wach Bataillon* from Amersfoort, reached Ede and established his headquarters in Hotel-Pension De Langenberg on Arnhemseweg just opposite Simon Stevin barracks. The *Ortskommandant* informed him about *'die eingesetzten Kräfte'* (the deployment of the forces) and their positions and ordered him to take command of all units. As the *Wach Bataillon* lacked NCOs the *Ortskommandant* decided to second seventy-five men to this battalion. In the course of the night they were to be split up over all companies of the *Wach Bataillon*.[53]

In the early evening the so-called *Jagdkommando* of the *Wach Bataillon* from Amersfoort was the first to report at De Langenberg. This unit was also called '*Spielmannszug*'(band of musicians) because it was made up out of drummers and buglers of the SS *Wach Bataillon*. They formed a regular reconnaissance unit of about thirty men and had come to Ede in requisitioned lorries. Since the early days of the *Wach Bataillon* their main task had been to hunt down and capture escaped prisoners of the Amersfoort concentration camp and they were also instructed to search all areas where airplanes or crews had landed. The fighting strength of these musicians was not very impressive and their commander was SS Sergeant Drum-Major Sackel.[54]

The *Jagdkommando* was ordered to reconnoitre the Ede-Arnhem road and to penetrate into the woods east of Zuid Ginkel Café. Sackel and his men took their bicycles and rode in an easterly direction. At the edge of the woods they were intercepted by No. 4 Platoon A Company and after some machine gun bursts a number of SS men was killed or wounded. Sergeant Sackel was severely wounded and died at a hospital in Apeldoorn. The others managed to escape and many of them deserted. In the end only four men returned to their headquarters in De Langenberg to report on the events.

In the evening the German troops were reinforced by the *4. Kompanie* of the *Wach Bataillon* from Amersfoort. It was the first of five companies that were to follow and it arrived together with a section of heavy arms. Only the *2. Kompanie* had a few vehicles at their disposal and horses drew the equipment of the others. By absence of the *2. Kompanie* the commanding officer of the *4. Kompanie*, Captain Bartsch, had managed to get hold of the vehicles of the former. The disadvantage for the *4. Kompanie* was that it was the first to go into action against the British.

At that moment the Germans still thought that the airborne

De Langenberg Hotel-Pension on Arnhemseweg at Ede. In the afternoon of 17 September 1944 it was the first command post of the ss Wach Bataillon 3 from Amersfoort. (PHOTO: ARCHIVES SOCIETY 'OLD EDE', NO. 320689)

forces would move forward to the west along the Ede-Arnhem road and had no idea of their exact position. However, the flat and open terrain on both sides of this road did not suit a daylight crossing and therefore the commanding officer of the *Wach Bataillon* decided to cross Ginkel Heath in the dark for an attack on the British.

Helle then made the mistake of deploying his battalion in parts against an enemy of whose strength and positions he was not exactly aware. Immediately after the *4. Kompanie* had reported itself on the spot, Helle started to execute his battle plan. Instead of waiting for the others to arrive he only deployed one fifth of his battalion, which resulted in the first of four nighttime attacks.

The *4. Kompanie* received the same orders as the *Jagdkommando*, i.e. to follow the Ede-Arnhem road and to clear the area both to the north and to the south of the road to the edge of the woods beyond Zuid Ginkel Café.

At about 20.45 hours No. 4 Platoon A Company 7 KOSB observed hostile troop movements along the Arnhem road opposite the café.

At about seventy yards to the east of the café the platoon had positioned an anti-tank gun. The British shot flares into the dark and managed to inflict heavy losses on both Germans and men of the Dutch SS, which prevented the *4. Kompanie* of the *Wach Bataillon* to reach the edge of the woods. For the time being the airborne troops had managed to consolidate their positions around the heath.

In the dark many SS troops deserted. The following day 'some of them returned to their units full of remorse'.[55]

Around midnight a patrol of B Company 7 KOSB managed to approach both Simon Stevin and Elias Beeckman barracks up to a distance of approximately fifty yards. However, they could not proceed beyond the gun position southeast of Simon Stevin barracks. Next the commanding officer of the barracks reinforced the *Schiffs-Stamm-Abteilung* with fifteen men of the *7. Kompanie* to better secure this 'front sector'.

The *Gefechtsbericht* (war diary) of the *Ortskommandant* mentioned twenty-five killed and sixty wounded on the German side.[56] The Roll of Honour mentioned seven British killed.[57]

In his summary of hostilities on 17 September Von Tettau wrote in his headquarters on Grebbeberg that 6./14. *Schiffs-Stamm-Abteilung* had reached the eastern edge of Bennekom that evening and that the *SS Wach Bataillon 3* had been deployed along the Ede-Arnhem road. He also mentioned that units of the *Artillerie Regiment 184* and defenders of Ede town had taken up their assigned positions. The general proudly announced that '*feindliche Vorstösse in westlicher Richtung*' (enemy advances to the west) had been prevented.[58] He could not know that the British never had the intention to push on in a westerly direction.

3. Monday, 18 September 1944: D + 1

THE PUSH FOR ARNHEM ROAD BRIDGE

Early that morning the 1st and 3rd Battalion of the 1st Parachute Brigade attempted to reach the road bridge at Arnhem once more. The 3rd Battalion under command of Lieutenant Colonel Fitch, of which C Company had managed to join the 2nd Battalion under command of Lieutenant Colonel Frost via another route the previous evening, started to move in the direction of Arnhem through Oosterbeek-Zuid and Oosterbeek Laag Station at 04.30 hours. The strong German line of defence halted their advance at the Rijnpaviljoen Hotel (see map no. 2).

The 1st Battalion under command of Lieutenant Colonel Dobie, whose advance was blocked at the Amsterdamseweg, moved via a southerly route to Oosterbeek. Via the northern and eastern edges of Oosterbeek the battalion took the same route as the 3rd, but also their advance was finally halted at the St Elisabeth's Hospital by the superior strength of the Germans.

THE ACTIONS OF THE WESTGRUPPE

Under cover of darkness the SS *Ausbildungs Bataillon Eberwein* reached the Grebbeberg. It was ordered to advance to the railway line south of Ginkel Heath via Wageningen and Bennekom and to join the defensive line at Ede. During the night the *10. Schiffs-Stamm-Abteilung*, the regimental staff of Lippert's NCO School and a detachment of this training school, the SS *Bataillon Schulz*, also reported at Von Tettau's headquarters and were directed to their positions in accordance with the outlined strategy.

Despite a lot of casualties Von Tettau's attack east of Wageningen managed to make some progress on the morning of 18 September. The SS NCO School drove the British out of Renkum and pushed on towards Heelsum where, together with the *Fliegerhorst Bataillon* from Soesterberg, it attacked the British at LZ-Z and DZ-X on Renkum Heath. Meanwhile *6./14. Schiffs-Stamm-Abteilung* was deployed east of Renkum and the *SS Bataillon Schulz* carried out an attack on Heelsum. At the same time the *Artillerie Regiment 184* had taken up positions in the woods near Bennekom on the western flank of this SS Battalion.

B Company of the 1st Battalion The Border Regiment, which had taken up positions along the Rhine south of Renkum, was under continuous attack by the *10. Schiffs-Stamm-Abteilung* and at approximately 15.00 hours the Germans managed to take the Renkum brickyard.

At the same time Eberwein's *SS Ausbildungs Bataillon* reached Bennekom to clear the Ede-Arnhem railway line.[1]

THE SITUATION AT GINKEL HEATH PRIOR TO THE ARRIVAL OF 4TH PARACHUTE BRIGADE

Around midnight the *3. Kompanie* of the *Wach Bataillon* under Hink arrived and Helle decided to deploy this detachment of Dutch SS immediately. It was to cross the heath to the right of the *4. Kompanie* and parallel to the trunk road. The advance of both companies was supported by half-tracks (see map no.4).

When the SS units reached the edge of the woods the British continuously shot flares to have a clear field of fire and at approximately 04.00 hours both companies had only managed to reach the northeastern part of the heath. Both in the middle of their front line and on their right flank the British resistance was so fierce that the ground gained had to be abandoned and the Dutch SS got stuck somewhere on the heath. The frontal night attack on the British

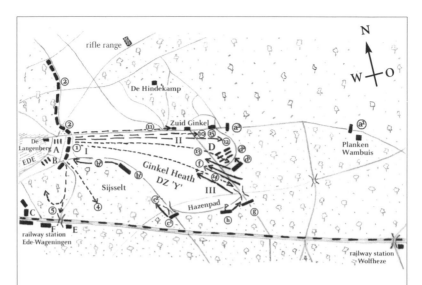

Map 4:   Battle positions at Ginkel Heath 18 September 1944.

A = Simon Stevin barracks
B = Elias Beeckman barracks
C = Maurits- en Johan Willem
     Friso barracks
D = Work camp 't Wijde Veld
E = Signal box19A
F = ENKA rayon works

British battle positions and patrols 7th Battalion KOSB
a¹ = headquarters A company
a² = no. 4 platoon A company
b¹ = battle position B company
b² = patrol B company
c¹ = battle position C company
c² = patrol C company
d¹ = battle position D company
d² = patrol D company
f = last Britsh attack prior to the landings
g = battle position Staff Company
h = headquarters 7 KOSB

German battle positions and patrols
1 = battle positions 7.Stammkompanie
2 = 2 sections 7.Stammkompanie
4 = Stammkompanie 20.Schiffs-
     Stamm-Abteilung
5 = 2 Wehrmacht artillery batteries
10 = 4.Kompanie SS Wach Bataillon 3
11 = 1.Kompanie SS Wach Bataillon 3
12 = 3.Kompanie SS Wach Bataillon 3
13 = 5.Kompanie SS Wach Bataillon 3
14 = 6.Kompanie SS Wach Bataillon 3
15 = section heavy arms SS Wach
     Bataillon 3

Drop zone 4th Parachute Brigade
I   = RV (RendezVous) 156 Battalion
II = RV (RendezVous) 10th Battalion
III = RV (RendezVous) 11th Battalion

Zuid Ginkel Café. At the moment of the landings of 4th Parachute Brigade it was used as command post by ss Wach Bataillon 3. (PHOTO: ARCHIVES SOCIETY 'OLD EDE')

positions had failed and both sides reported a number of casualties.

During that same night the Germans moved the headquarters of the *Wach Bataillon* from Hotel Pension De Langenberg to Zuid Ginkel Café, north of the heath.

In the meantime the *1. Kompanie* had reinforced this battalion. The *3.* and *4. Kompanie* of the *Wach Bataillon* covered the front of the café while the *1. Kompanie* was kept in reserve in the woods to the west. The reason for this is still totally unclear as this last mentioned company took up positions at the flank that was not threatened at all. Most likely Helle felt that his headquarters could do with some additional protection.

The detachment carrying heavy arms was directed to the terrain north of the road and to the east of the café from which position they started shelling the British No. 4 Platoon A Company early that morning.

Meanwhile about 140 men of the *6. Kompanie* of the *SS Wach*

Bataillon under command of Captain Fernau had also reached the front and the Germans now attempted to push on to the southern edge of Ginkel Heath.

The company was to try and encircle the British positions by traversing the woods and linking up with the SS *Ausbildungs Bataillon* that was on the move from Bennekom to the railway line east of Ede. In the early hours of the morning the 6. *Kompanie* was ordered to advance in a southerly direction and not much later it was to discover that the British also occupied this side of the heath.

That morning the attack began at 05.00 hours. Ten minutes earlier all available guns had opened preliminary fire on the British positions. The guns of the 3. and 4. *Kompanie*, viz. three 37 mm anti-tank guns, six grenade launchers and some machine-guns were brought forward. On the trunk road the Germans deployed armoured cars whose searchlights tried to spot the positions of 7 KOSB in the woods, which were subsequently strafed by their 20 mm guns and machine guns.

Meanwhile the German and Dutch SS infantry units tried to infiltrate the British positions and attempted to get a foothold at the edge of the woods.[2] No. 4 Platoon A Company in particular had to endure heavy shelling. It withstood three of such attacks and suffered severe losses in the process. Lieutenant Colonel Payton Reid noted in his report that 'the Hun is a very determined fighter'.[3]

How resolute the Germans were, the British found out when they were forced to evacuate the woods south of the Ede-Arnhem road opposite the café. No. 4 Platoon A Company had to retreat in the direction of the Planken Wambuis and join the rest of the company and leave its 6-pounder anti-tank gun behind. The Germans and Dutch SS were at the heels of the airborne troops and repeatedly attacked the positions of A Company. However, it stood firm and succeeded in inflicting heavy losses on the enemy and take a number of prisoners.

Elsewhere along Ginkel Heath the companies of the *Wach Bataillon* met with heavy resistance from the airborne troops, which were entrenched along the entire length and breadth of the woods. They finally managed to reach the fly-over underneath the '*Hazenpad*' on the southeastern edge of the heath, but at the other end of the ten yards long tunnel they were driven back by machine-gun fire issued by men from the British battalion headquarters, which exchange of fire resulted in twelve killed and a number of wounded Germans and Dutch SS.

Various parts of the heath were set alight by both German and British mortar bombs and Very lights.

When being interrogated by the Dutch police after the war the adjutant of the SS *Wach Bataillon* mentioned fierce man-to-man fighting whereby 'the enemy used knifes and our troops fought with entrenching tools and bayonets'.[4] This was probably slightly exaggerated as there was no mention of this in any of the postwar interviews with British soldiers.

Meanwhile Kühne and his *5. Kompanie* of the *Wach Bataillon* had also reached the heath. He was immediately ordered to close the gap between the *6.* and *3. Kompanie*. While the British continued to shoot flares it crossed the heath and the bicycle track south of the sheepfold. Despite the fact that the whole area was lit up the Germans and Dutch SS managed to reach the sheds of the work camp 't Wijde Veld.

Shortly afterwards around fifty totally surprised men of the British D Company were taken prisoner. Under cover of the night they had been surrounded without noticing any danger. Somehow the position and strength of the platoon had been passed on to the enemy, possibly by means of 'a hidden telephone'.[5]

The *5. Kompanie* did not manage to gain any further ground as the British fire from the woods was too well directed. Nevertheless the Germans repeatedly tried to drive the airborne troops back.

The result of all these actions was that shortly after 05.00 hours the northeastern part of the heath was in hands of the Germans and the Dutch SS who subsequently attempted to push further ahead to the

south along the edge of the woods. There were a number of engagements in the woods, which went on almost the whole day prior to
the next landings. The British D Company in particular was
involved in this 'man-to-man' fighting.[6]

Moreover, it lay under constant fire from German heavy arms
which were positioned at the northern edge of the woods near the
trunk road and the position of D Company on the eastern side of
the heath became very precarious.

Due to the absence of proper communications all British actions
during the night lacked coordination. In most cases it had been little groups of men and individuals who had done their utmost to
protect their positions against hostile infiltration.

Early next morning headquarters 7 KOSB were therefore not
aware of what had happened during the previous night. The British
were left with the impression that the woods on the northeastern
edge of the Dz were still in German hands.

At 07.00 hours the commander of 7 KOSB therefore ordered a platoon of D Company to attack the enemy in the woods on the northeastern side of the heath and try to contact A Company in that section of the DZ. It was decided to use the position that was held by
the British in the work camp as base of operation. As the platoon
approached the camp four Borderers jumped over the wire fence
and at that same moment shots were exchanged. The SS personnel
of the 5. *Kompanie* spotted the airborne soldiers through the windows of one of the sheds. They immediately started firing straight
through all the windows and the huts. The civilians were having
breakfast and it was later said that 'those people were just eating and
they shot the eggs of the table!'[7] The occupants of the camp shout-
ed and screamed and after a British lieutenant had thrown a smoke
grenade the men of 7 KOSB retreated to the shelter of the trees.

Shortly afterwards the Germans ordered the evacuation of the
camp.

In the early hours of the morning the men of No. 3 Platoon 21st
Independent Parachute Company under the command of Lieute-

German forces on the Ede-Arnhem trunk road. These photos are stills taken from moving pictures taken on the morning of 18 September 1944. Bottom picture shows Ginkel Heath on the right.

(PHOTOS: AIRBORNE MUSEUM OOSTERBEEK, NO. AD-10 AND AL-10)

nant Ashmore arrived at Ginkel Heath. They had to mark the DZ for the next landings.[8]

The British captured at the work camp were moved to a field just north of the Ede-Arnhem road at a distance of approximately thirty yards to the west of the Zuid Ginkel Café and were marched to Ede shortly afterwards. This was not without any danger. During their march along the trunk road the men feared to be fired at by their comrades of B Company by mistake, which luckily did not happen. From their positions at the edge of De Sijsselt woods the troops of this company watched the men of D Company being led away, but they could not come to their rescue. Because of hostile fire it was impossible to cross the open terrain.

In the course of the morning these captured airborne troops were the first British, which the citizens of Ede saw at Hotel Welgelegen on Stationsweg. Instead of prisoners of war one had hoped to welcome victorious Tommies. The citizens of Ede were very disappointed and their hope of being liberated was soon thwarted.

At daybreak and after heavy shelling the Germans and Dutch SS once more attempted to attack in a southerly direction through the woods on the eastern side of the DZ. They were repelled once again and did not gain any further ground. Both sides reported a number of casualties.

Later that morning skirmishes were reported on the western side of the heath. After the early-morning mist had lifted men of B Company 7 KOSB saw a detachment of Germans riding to the 'front' on the trunk road 'on push-bikes and motorcycles'.[9] They were soon to find out that the enemy was nearer than they anticipated and the 'cyclists' did not get very far.

A few minutes later men of B Company, which were entrenched on the northern side of De Sijsselt woods, observed the approach of a German scout car. Immediately an anti-tank gun was brought into position and the first shot was a hit. Shortly afterwards three German armoured half tracks, equipped with 20 mm guns and carrying about fifteen men each, came under British fire on the trunk road and were put out of action. When the Germans jumped off the vehicles they were strafed by machine-gun fire which resulted in many of them killed and wounded.

British snipers were also deployed and these succeeded in putting five German motor orderlies out of action. The German ambulances that arrived to collect the dead and wounded were left undisturbed.[10]

The Germans finally pinpointed the British positions and in the course of the morning their line of fire became more direct. At the same time they tried to infiltrate B Company's lines through the dense woods of De Sijsselt.

A round of mortar grenades, which killed four Germans, repelled an attack by a German reconnaissance unit through the undergrowth along the edge of the heath. The British also reported some casualties i.e. two wounded and one killed. The last round fatally wounded Private Alexander McKay of the mortar crew. The grenade hit a branch and exploded above his head. His remains were found in De Sijsselt woods on 14 February 1946 and he was buried at the Algemene Begraafplaats (General Cemetery) in Ede.

An attack on a German machine gun position at the edge of the woods of De Sijsselt was also executed with mortar fire. B Company managed to knock it out and forced the Germans to retreat.[11] Meanwhile the British shelled the barracks with mortar rounds and strafed the grounds with machine guns. German snipers fired at the entrenched British, but were driven back soon afterwards.

During the ensuing standoff the Germans waited for the arrival of reinforcements while the British were waiting for the second lift, which according to the schedule was due to arrive at approximately 10.00 hours. Before the landings the airborne troops had to clear the heath from any enemy activity and push back the Germans as far as possible as even the RV of 10th Parachute Battalion, close to Zuid Ginkel Café, was still in German hands. Moreover, the café itself was used as headquarters of the SS Wach Bataillon. Therefore it was vital to drive the enemy from both the café and the adjoining

The grave of Private A. McKay on Algemene Begraafplaats in Ede. The epitaph reads:

> 'Dearer to us
> than words can tell
> was the son we lost
> and loved so well'

(PHOTO: AUTHOR)

Private Alexander McKay, 7th Battalion The King's
Own Scottish Borderers

(PHOTO: MUNICIPAL ARCHIVES, EDE, NO. 7610)

woods prior to the landing of 4th Parachute Brigade. However, the men of the Advance Party of this brigade, who had landed with the first lift, did not manage to clear the area. The only possibility to reach the café was through a combined attack from the southern and eastern positions round the heath. It was decided to postpone this attack until shortly before the actual landings. In case it should fail 10th Parachute Battalion would have to clear the RV on its own. In the war diary of the battalion it was noted that 'that was one exercise that we had not practised.'[12]

At the appointed hour of 10.00 hours no approaching planes were heard. The men of 7 KOSB and 21st Independent Parachute Company were ready for action, but no fixed bayonet charge was called for nor were the Pathfinders required to set up the marker panels and radio beacons. No Dakotas or other planes appeared above Ginkel Heath. However, the British around the DZs and LZs used on Sunday were shocked to suddenly notice a number of Messerschmitt fighters coming out of the sky. The airborne soldiers quickly ran for cover. They had been told that the *Luftwaffe* would not bother them and that the only airplanes they would see would be their own. Now this turned out to be quite another matter and about twenty to thirty ME-109s dived out of the skies 'with their guns blazing'.[13] LZ-X, where the gliders carrying vehicles and anti-tank guns of 4th Parachute Brigade were to land, was also strafed. Elsewhere four abandoned gliders went up in flames.

It was obvious that, contrary to German army headquarters, the command of the German *Luftwaffe* had apparently taken the operational plan or part of it, found near Vught the previous day, very serious. Approximately two hundred fighters had been directed to the British and American DZs and LZs to intercept the airfleet that was due to arrive that Monday.

Fortunately the take off of the second lift in England had been delayed for four to five hours. At the moment the second lift finally appeared above its DZs and LZs the German fighters had returned to their airfields to be refuelled.

What the Borderers on Ginkel Heath did not know was that the delay in England was caused by a rather thick early-morning mist and low clouds. The skies had finally cleared around 11.00 hours at which moment the all clear had been given. Shortly before the airborne troops near Ede had been informed by radio message from divisional headquarters that the landings had been delayed for a couple of hours.

Meanwhile the fighting around the heath continued. Towards noon a patrol of B Company from the western section of De Sijsselt woods managed to get within a very short distance of Simon Stevin barracks where they caused a lot of casualties. One British airborne soldier was killed during this action.

Early in the afternoon the Germans reinforced the frontline. Approximately fifty to sixty men started to dig in alongside the trunk road. They did not get the time to finish their job as the airborne soldiers of B Company managed to chase them off.

A few minutes later the British observed a German gun position on the open heath land opposite the trunk road. It was knocked out, as it would have been a great threat to the forthcoming landings.

B Company was also ordered to prevent German vehicles of using this road. After the successes of the morning the anti-tank gunners managed to hit another couple of German armoured cars and Lieutenant Carter noted in his personal diary: 'we added one or two more to the score.'[14]

The valiant actions of the men from B Company had secured their section of the 'front' for the safe landing of 4th Parachute Brigade. In this section the number of British casualties was limited to two killed and some wounded, which latter were safely taken to a field hospital.

C Company was assigned the southwestern section of Ginkel Heath, which part of the DZ had not seen any serious action prior to the landings. During the night both the British of C Company and the Germans had patrolled the area intensively and on the adjoining part of the heath there had been exchanges of fire with some small German units. During one of these skirmishes six Germans were taken prisoner. Only C Company 7 KOSB did not report any losses prior to the arrival of 4th Parachute Brigade.[15]

In the meantime increased German reconnaissance activities harassed the Borderers of D Company in the eastern section of Ginkel Heath at midday. At the edge of the woods Germans and Dutch SS advanced from all directions in a renewed effort to push back the British.

The Germans kept on bringing in reinforcements while the British did not have any reserves and their commander described the situation as 'extremely tricky'. The British positions threatened to be overrun and the airborne troops valiantly tried to make a stand.[16]

Both sides deployed all available men and weapons and ultimately the British managed to prevent a German breakthrough. However, they could not stop an enemy advance from the edge of the woods further south. Shortly afterwards the Germans pulled back the majority of their forces to the northeastern part of the heath and the adjoining woods. From their new positions in this section of the DZ the Germans were now able to cover the landing of 4th Parachute Brigade, which created an extremely threatening situation.

THE SECOND LIFT

The next phase of Operation Market started early in the morning of 18 September. The second lift was to carry substantial reinforcements for the 101st US Airborne Division to an area near Eindhoven, for the 82nd US Airborne Division to Nijmegen and Grave and for the 1st British Airborne Division to Arnhem.

After a delay of almost five hours take-off commenced at 11.20 hours when Dakotas, Albemarles and Halifaxes, many of them towing gliders, departed from Saltby, Spanhoe and Cottesmore airfields in eastern England. 126 Dakotas finally took 4th Parachute Brigade under the command of Brigadier John Hackett and incorporating 10th, 11th and 156 Parachute Battalions to Ginkel Heath. The brigade's heavy equipment viz. Bren carriers, jeeps, two anti-tank batteries (Royal Artillery) and supplies were carried to LZ-X near Renkum by gliders.

Twenty-seven fighter squadrons consisting of Typhoons, Mustangs, Tempests and Spitfires escorted the air fleet. The counteractions of the German *Luftwaffe* were limited to an attempt by approximately ninety fighters to attack the allied air armada, but they did not match the superior numbers of the British and American fighter planes.

German flak was much heavier than during the first lift. The Germans had come to the simple conclusion that reinforcements of the airborne divisions could only be flown in from the south and west and it was on those approaches to the DZs and LZs that they had rushed to built up their anti-aircraft defences, which were concentrated near Randwijk, just south of the river Rhine.

At his headquarters in Doetinchem the commander of II SS *Panzer Korps*, General Bittrich, was in constant touch with the *Luftwaffe's* intelligence staff, which mainly got its information from the Channel ports that were still occupied by the Germans. Three quarters of an hour prior to the actual landings the Germans knew that the allied reinforcements were on their way whereupon a mobile SS reserve unit and a number of anti-aircraft guns, that were deployed near the Arnhem road bridge, were immediately directed to the LZs.

Despite the heavy flak the American formations flew steadily on and kept their Dakotas in formation maintaining their course and speed. Many planes were hit, but the crews managed to keep them in the air. Altogether six planes were shot down before reaching the DZs. Two Dakotas went down over Rhenen of which one crashed west and the other east of the river Grift.[17] During the forced landing one of these planes hit a power line and exploded.[18] Elsewhere

General B.L. Montgomery (left), Major General R.E. Urquhart (right) and Brigadier J.W. Hackett (middle) after inspecting 4th Parachute Brigade at the sports ground of Oakham School on 8 March 1944.

in the formation a plane received a direct hit and went down in flames. It carried half of 156 Battalion's machine gun platoon. The total number of killed was twenty-four, which included the pilot and crew and eighteen paratroopers. The pilots of the other five planes managed to drop their sticks of the 10th and 11th Parachute Battalion before having to make a forced landing.

Some of the gliders also did not reach their destination. One glider crashed during the start. Eight glider pilots had to make forced landings in England and two others ditched in the North Sea. About twelve gliders went down over Holland. One tug plane was shot down and some others were badly damaged.

All these accidents cost the lives of thirty-one paratroopers and seventeen crew members while eleven crew members and approximately seventy-three paratroopers escaped certain death.[19] At least twenty-four damaged American Dakotas returned safely to their bases in England.

One plane managed to reach England after its pilot was killed by flak. The second navigator did a terrific job. Although he had never flown a plane before, he succeeded to cast off the tow rope and put it safely on the ground.[20]

THE LANDING ON GINKEL HEATH

In order to protect the landing of the second lift the British at the edges of the heath had decided to aim their four 3-inch mortars at the enemy's stronghold and to cover the German positions with a thick smokescreen. When at approximately 15.00 hours the hum of approaching aircraft could be heard in the distance, there was a temporary cease-fire. At that moment both northern and eastern sections of the DZ were still in hands of the Germans.

Minutes before the landings, men of 7 KOSB led by their commanding officer began a last frantic attack from the southeast section of the heath to drive the Germans and Dutch SS from the DZ and the surrounding area. They managed to regain full control over the southeastern section of the heath, but the enemy remained lodged in drainage ditches, groves, and shrubbery. At the same time the fire on the heath spread out.

The clearance of the southeastern part of the DZ regretfully caused some British losses. The total number of casualties of 7 KOSB was two officers and at least thirteen other ranks.

Under steady hostile fire men of No. 3 Platoon 21st Independent Parachute Company started to spread out the marker panels, i.e. a white 'Y' indicating the actual DZ and a red 'T' denoting the wind direction. They also put up Eureka radio beacons on the 'Hazenpad', the current motorway A 12.

At the same time the Advance Party of 4th Parachute Brigade lit green and blue smoke canisters at the edge of the heath to indicate the appointed RVs.

Wave after wave of aircraft appeared on the horizon over the south-western corner of Ginkel Heath. The low flying allied air armada of 120 Dakotas approached over the railway line and the 'Hazenpad' in a V for Victory formation. The American pilots brought in their planes in groups of nine at a height of approximately six hundred feet and approached the DZ with great precision. After the first flight of thirty-six C-47 Dakotas the remaining aircraft, escorted by Spitfires and Typhoons, followed in batches at one minute intervals.

From their positions in the woods, on the heath, from the work camp and from under the trees along the Ede-Arnhem road the Germans and Dutch SS used all available small arms, such as rifles, machine guns and bren guns seized from the British, to fire at the passing Dakotas. Everywhere mortar grenades exploded.

Meanwhile a stiff breeze had started to blow and slowly a bluish grey haze, which pungent smell was a mixture of gunsmoke and burning heather, darkened a big part of the heath.

Several Dakotas were hit. One C-47 received a direct hit over the DZ, caught fire and stood 'ablaze from nose to tail'. The airplane lost height rapidly, but the pilot managed to keep his 'crate' in the air enabling the sixteen paratroopers to jump. A few moments later it hit the ground and exploded in a great white ball of flame. All crew members were killed. Two Typhoons dived down and knocked out the flak guns with their rockets.

The paratroopers stood in the open doorways of the Dakotas and waited for the green light. They saw the burning heath below them and heard the firing from automatic and other firearms. The DZ was partially hidden from their view and the whole scene made the impression of a pitched battle. They had been told that the landing area was supposed to be quiet.

Approximately two thousand paratroopers – a more precise esti-mate being 1,914 - of the 4th Parachute Brigade jumped in the midst of this inferno.[21] According to a report from the US Air Force 'they made their drop in a shower of tracers'.[22] The time was 15.09 hours. The American aircrews flew in very tight formations and therefore the dropping did not take more than nine minutes. Seven men were unable to jump because they were hit during the approach or got entangled in the static lines of their parachutes.

The first to jump were men of 156 Battalion. They were to rendezvous in the most westerly section of the heath. Next to follow were both other battalions. 11th Battalion landed in the southern corner of the DZ and 10th Parachute Battalion jumped over the northern part of the heath, opposite Zuid Ginkel Café. The men of 7 KOSB gave a sigh of relief. In the words of their commanding officer the landings to them were 'an amazing sight and a terrific relief'.[23] After nearly twenty-four hours of almost continuous fierce fighting it must have been a fascinating spectacle and a tremendous load of their minds to see scores of aircraft dropping the men of 4th Parachute Brigade, who came down in long rows of green coloured parachutes.

The Germans and Dutch SS were aiming at the doorways of the Dakotas, hoping to hit the first man in the stick so that the remainder could not jump or causing a delay, which would result in paratroopers landing in the trees on the other side of the trunk road. Several paratroopers were hit in the air and others fired their sten guns and threw hand-grenades at the enemies below them.

Because of the stiff breeze some paratroopers ended up in the woods and were fired at by the retreating Germans and Dutch SS. Others hit the trees near the German headquarters at Zuid Ginkel Café, which most of them did not survive.

In his report the German *Ortskommandant* wrote that part of his forces had put up a plucky resistance. From a 'reinforced position' on the north side of the road men of his own 7. *Kompanie* and also from other companies had defended themselves bravely against the British paratroopers. The commanding officer further wrote that 'after his first battle experience a raw recruit boasted of having killed five paratroopers still hanging on their parachutes. Afterwards this recruit, who was an opera singer in civilian life, could not believe that he had been able to kill paratroopers who were still in the air.'[24] The question remains whether this music lover spoke the truth as the speed of a descending paratrooper and the short time available make it next to impossible to knock out five paratroopers in a row.

In the same report the *Ortskommandant* rather enthusiastically wrote about the performance of several of his troops. Obviously he wanted to conceal from his superiors that the majority of his forces had stopped fighting after having 'performed' for a short time only.

The paratroopers, who managed to reach the ground, were fired at by mortars, automatic and other light weapons. Several were hit before they could strip off their parachute-harnesses. Immediately upon landing on the ground many had to run over the burning heath in order to save their skin, while the ground was covered with duds.

One paratrooper was hit in both legs and was unable to move. When the burning heather had reached him and set his ammunition pouches on fire, he took his revolver and shot himself in the head.

Other paratroopers had to run for cover. One of them later said: 'We dug in and the whole thing turned out to be a massacre.'[25]

In his book entitled *It Never Snows in September* Colonel Kershaw writes that 'Ginkel Heath was a scene of utter pandemonium'.[26] Middlebrook quotes the words used by an American C-47 navigator to describe the situation: 'I don't know what hell will be like, but I think we got a preview. Earlier groups had already dropped and the DZ was a solid ball of fire. At the command to jump, our troops had exited from the plane without any hesitation. My admiration, already at an extremely high level where paratroopers were concerned, went even higher as these brave men dropped into that preview of hell.'[27]

Despite the fierce enemy resistance and thanks to the preliminary actions by 7 KOSB the British did not panic.

18 September 1944. Ginkel Heath just before the landings of 4th Parachute Brigade. Due to German and British mortar fire par middle the 'Hazenpad' (A12) under construction.

...eath is burning. Top right are Zuid Ginkel Café and the Ede-Arnhem road. Middle right the work camp 't Wijde Veld and bottom

(PHOTO: COURTESY OF THE AIRBORNE MUSEUM OOSTERBEEK)

73

In their headquarters at Zuid Ginkel Café the Germans heard the airplanes coming over and saw the paratroopers coming down. Some of them even landed in front of their command post. The men of 10th Parachute Battalion, who had landed nearest to their RV, took cover behind the southern bank of the trunk road. A little later they started clearing the woods on the other side and stormed the café.

The commanding officer of the *Wach Bataillon* was still asleep and was awakened by his adjutant. When some British paratroopers looked through the windows, the Germans rushed through the backdoor and ran away through the garden. The commander and his adjutant followed their example. At the fence they got entangled in the barbed wire, but in the end they managed to get away unhurt.

The reserve company and its Dutch commander, which were to defend the headquarters, were nowhere to be seen.

All this should not have happened much later. The German officer in charge of the heavy guns watched the British approach the café, turned his anti-tank gun around and started shelling his own command post. Shortly afterwards the gun was knocked out by the British and the gun crew also fled to a safer place. Most Germans and Dutch SS retreated towards Hindekamp Farm.

The fighting near the café only caused 'light casualties' and ten Germans were taken prisoner.[28]

The Germans and Dutch SS still on the heath were caught between 7 KOSB to the south and the paratroopers who had just landed behind them. Even before the last paratroopers had hit the ground, they either had fled or were happy to surrender.

Despite the flak and the problems during the dropping ninety percent of the paratroopers managed to land at the appointed zone. D Company 10th Parachute Battalion landed at approximately fifteen hundred yards from the DZ and was fortunate to reach headquarters shortly afterwards.

Because one flight of nine Dakotas had been separated from the main force their paratroopers were dropped north of the DZ.

Seventeen men of 10th Parachute Battalion landed miles way from the DZ and were engaged in several skirmishes. In the end only six of them managed to survive and were able to escape to England with help from the Dutch resistance.

At least three detachments of paratroopers were involved in the most northerly landing. Eighty of them landed near De Zanding in Otterlo and part of these men were taken to Planken Wambuis Café by members of the Dutch resistance. Two of these groups, totalling thirty-one men, were of 133 Parachute Field Ambulance, Royal Army Medical Corps.

Because paratroopers in another plane did not jump at the right moment, they landed in the trees far off the heath. Several of them landed amidst a German platoon that fled away. A few minutes later the British came across an abandoned lorry full of weapons and ammunition. They drove it to Zuid Ginkel Café. The same lorry was later used to transport a number of wounded to Oosterbeek.[29]

Some containers with weapons, ammunition and food also over-shot the DZ and ended up in trees.

There were a great number of casualties. In addition to the killed and the severely and slightly wounded as result of the hostilities, there were also several paratroopers with broken legs or ankles. Immediately after the landings 133 Parachute Field Ambulance put up a Dressing Station in Zuid Ginkel Café. According to the RAMC report the situation on the spot was 'one of absolute chaos'.[30] Because of the great number of casualties not all wounded could be properly attended to. Moreover, two sticks of the Royal Army Medical Corps had landed near Otterlo. At the assembly point it turned out that the second in command, some medical officers and approximately forty other medical staff were missing. None of them managed to reach the division. Because of this the medical unit had to do without one of their surgeons, two medical officers and several orderlies.

After the fighting had stopped medics and stretcher-bearers

searched the heath. Upturned rifles stuck in the ground marked the positions of the wounded, which were to be picked up at a later moment. Regrettably, some of them were beyond any help. They had not been able to move and were burnt 'when the heather around them caught fire'.[31]

Besides all the suffering and carnage that took place on Ginkel Heath, there was also mention of some remarkable events. Immediately after having landed two paratroopers were busy trying to shoot a large hare.

Another had a small box containing a homing pigeon and a little bag of birdseed hanging from one of his battledress straps. He was hit in mid air and would later say: 'At a certain moment I was left with half the box and the birdseed only. I think the bird made a flying start somewhere between a height of four hundred feet and the ground'.[32]

During the jump Brigadier Hackett lost his walking stick. Immediately upon landing he started to look for it and kept on looking even when two SS wanted to surrender. He kept them waiting till he had found his cane. Meanwhile the heath was burning and the men of his 4th Parachute Brigade landed in a rain of bullets coming from all sorts of weapons. Hackett later recalled that 'two of the enemy gave themselves up to me about two minutes after I was out of my parachute-harness. I had a couple of prisoners even before I had a command-post'.[33] This number would grow to six before he had reached the RV.

However, it remains curious that the commanding officer of the brigade spent some time retrieving his walking stick in the midst of a battle and by doing so took a very great risk of being hit and put out of action.

At the RVs it turned out that on account of the planes, which were lost and the dropping beyond the appointed zone, each battalion was missing a number of officers and other ranks.

When 156 Battalion reached its RV, two officers and one hundred

Approximately 80 paratroopers landed near De Zanding in Otterlo. They were greeted by cheering citizens. The photos were taken on Arnhemseweg.

(TOP AND MIDDLE PHOTOS: COURTESY OF MR J.W. VAN DER MEIJDEN, OTTERLO — BOTTOM PHOTO: MR B. SLOOF, EDE)

Paratrooper with cylinder for
a carrier-pigeon.

(COURTESY OF THE IMPERIAL WAR
MUSEUM, LONDON, IN: ARCHIVES AIR-
BORNE MUSEUM OOSTERBEEK)

other ranks were missing. They were reported as 'casualties and
stragglers'of which twenty-five men were wounded during the
dropping or the landing, the so-called 'jumping casualties'.[34] Moreover, one plane was lost during the fly-in. It meant a total loss of
battle strength of almost twenty percent.

The report of 10th Parachute Battalion mentions twenty-five
'jumping-casualties', one airplane missing and 'some casualties in
the air'. The report of 11th Parachute Battalion states three aircraft
lost during the fly-in.

In total 4th Parachute Brigade had lost over two hundred killed,
wounded or missing, which accounted for approximately ten percent of its operational strength at a moment when the advance to
Arnhem had yet to start.[35]

The men of the 6. *Kompanie* of the Dutch SS *Wach Bataillon* were taken prisoner. The 1. *Kompanie* had fled and the 3., 4., and 5. *Kompanie* tried to escape to the north, but the majority of the men were either killed, wounded or taken prisoner.

The commanders of these units did not fare much better. Kühne had 'a nervous breakdown', fled and was relieved of his command. He was captured together with Bartsch and Fernau. Hink was severely wounded and transported to Ede.

Many captured 'Germans' were interrogated by the Dutch commando Beekmeijer, who as an interpreter for 7 KOSB, was given the task of gathering as much information as possible. He also interrogated a number of men from the *Wach Bataillon* of which he had to admit after the war: 'To my great shame I noticed that many of these 'Huns' were Dutch and came from the Amersfoort concentration camp'.[36]

It is unknown how many men of the *Wach Bataillon* were either killed, wounded, deserted or survived the battle for Ginkel Heath. When being interrogated by the police after the war the commander of the battalion testified that after the Battle of Arnhem it had counted forty-two killed, 124 heavily wounded and 120 missing. In his statement his adjutant mentioned more than sixty killed, three hundred seriously wounded and over 150 deserters, which never returned while the others who 'disappeared' during the fighting were located at a later date and subsequently punished. In total the *Wach Bataillon* lost more than half of its men.[37]

The exact number of Germans killed in the fighting is also unknown. On 17 September the *Ortskommandant* reported twenty-five killed and sixty wounded, but on the following day his *Gefechtsbericht* only mentioned '*mit Sicherheit festgestellte Verluste unbekannt*' (the exact number of losses is unknown).[38]

Approximately twenty-five Germans were buried in the grounds of Simon Stevin barracks, but most of the men were buried on the spot where they were killed. In 1948 a total of ninety-five Germans were buried in a mass grave at the Algemene Begraafplaats at Ede. It is unknown how many of these men were killed during the Battle

Ginkel Heath shortly after the landings of 4th Parachute Brigade on Monday 18 September 1944. In the front Brigadier John W. Hackett en route to the Brigade's RV. Captain Jasper Booty of 4th Parachute Brigade HQ illegally took this picture.   (PHOTO: ARCHIVES SOCIETY 'OLD EDE', NO. 17F711)

for Ginkel Heath.[39] Their remains were later transferred to the German military cemetery at Ysselsteyn in the province of Limburg.

The losses of 4th Parachute Brigade would have been much greater if the men of 7 KOSB and No. 3 Platoon of the 21st Independent Parachute Company had not cleared most of the heath shortly before its landing. The fighting had been of an extremely fierce and tenacious nature. 7 KOSB and the Pathfinders had acquitted themselves of their task in the most excellent way. Given the circumstances the losses of 4th Parachute Brigade were reduced to an absolute minimum. In 'The official Account of the British Airborne Divisions' entitled *By Air to Battle*, it is stated as follows: '7 KOSB lost a certain number of men holding the DZs and LZs, but the battalion so effectively accomplished its task that the casualties among the 4th Parachute Brigade on landing were very small'. The report comes to the conclusion that the landing therefore could be executed without excessive difficulties.[40] According to the report of the US Air Force 'the dropping was rightly regarded as very successful'.[41]

After the fighting had ended Hackett thanked the commanding officer of 7 KOSB 'for getting the paratroops such a good landing'.[42]

The level of intensity of the fighting during the dropping and the total of British losses are subject to various interpretations. The war diary of 10th Parachute Battalion states: 'When the battalion arrived there was a pitched battle going on across the DZ.' (....) There was an 'intense opposition'.[43] The report of 11th Parachute Battalion endorses this conclusion and states: 'The resistance was considerably stronger than expected'.[44] Major Waddy said that it was 'a difficult arrival'.[45] The report of the 21st Independent Parachute Company states that the 'drop was made under heavy groundfire'.[46] In his diary the commanding officer of 4th Parachute Brigade, Brigadier John Hackett, wrote that during the landings his men were met by 'considerable small arms fire'.[47]

However, the battle report of the 1st British Airborne Division states that 4th Parachute Brigade did not experience any significant opposition during its landing.[48]

In the war diary of 7 KOSB it is mentioned that the actions of the battalion enabled the paratroopers to land 'almost entirely free from hostile small arms fire'.[49] The last statement may seem a little bit too favourable and gives the impression that the diarist wished the contribution of 7 KOSB, however important, to appear too manifestly. His report probably formed the basis of the divisional report.

In their book entitled *De Slag bij Arnhem* (The Battle of Arnhem) the authors, Messrs Bauer and Boeree, come to the following conclusion: 'The actual landing was indeed not entirely unopposed. The SS battalion (...) put up some resistance, but (...) after a short while fled in total confusion.'[50] The last may be true, but the authors' conclusion that the dropping 'did not go unopposed' is an understatement that does not justify the events on Ginkel Heath.

In the summary of his book entitled *De verloren slag* (The Devil's

Birthday) Colonel Powell puts the events into perspective and he probably comes closest to the truth when he says that 'although it resulted in a number of dead and wounded, the reception was rather spectacular instead of dangerous.'[51] The actions of 7 KOSB prior to the landings did indeed reduce the risks for Brigadier Hackett's brigade, but how great the actual danger was, can only be deduced from the probable number of casualties.

The records are also not clear with regard to the actual number of casualties. According to the RAMC report there were a 'lot of casualties'.[52] However, in *By Air to Battle* the number is being put in perspective when it reads: 'The arrival of the second lift occurred without any serious losses.'[53]

This seems all rather confusing. These different interpretations are determined by the moment of publication of the various reports, books and articles. *By Air to Battle* was published in 1945 and Boeree used the war diary of 7 KOSB, which was also written shortly after the war. At that moment in time one did not have access to the data, which we can peruse today.

Apart from the authors' personal interpretation of events it does matter whether a detachment of paratroopers landed near Zuid Ginkel Café, in the middle of burning heather or in the most westerly section of the DZ, where it was relatively 'quiet'.

The fact that the Germans and notably men of the Dutch SS quickly fled from the scene of the battle or surrendered when they realised that they were facing superior forces may also have influenced this appraisal.[54] The actual fighting during and after the dropping took a comparative short period of time.

The disparities in the assessment of the actual losses are strongly related to what one beforehand considers as an acceptable number of casualties in this kind of operation. It must also be taken into account that the first reports were indeed based on details available at that moment.

The only proper assessment of the British losses on Ginkel Heath can be made by 133 Parachute Field Ambulance. Its report is also the most recent and was published in 1999. Unfortunately, it also does

The provisional mass grave on Amsterdamseweg east of the municipal timber yard. On 24, 25 and 26 September 1944 thirty-five allied and eight German soldiers were buried here. Thirty-eight of them were killed during the fighting on Ginkel Heath. The other five were RAF crew members who were killed when their plane crashed near Planken Wambuis. This picture was taken by Sergeant Hewitt on 18 April 1945.

not contain exact figures and confines itself to 'numerous casualties'.

With regard to the number of killed in the British army units, which were involved in the Battle for Ginkel Heath, the Roll of Honour of 1999 gives a total of ninety-seven for 18 September.[55] However, this figure includes men killed elsewhere that day and paratroopers who lost their lives when their planes were shot down.

Middlebrook comes to the conclusion that during the landings and the subsequent fighting the British lost four officers and approximately twenty-eight other ranks.[56]

This figure is most probably incorrect. If one adds the number on the Roll of Honour to that on a list made up by an undertaker in Ede, who in cooperation with the Red Cross buried a number of

Aerial photo of the provisional mass grave on Amsterdamseweg Ede-Arnhem. The two small white rectangles on the east side of the road indicate the mass grave (See arrow). A little above the middle of this picture on the right of the trunk road is the municipal timber yard. The picture was taken by the Allies on 23 December 1944.

British, the total number of killed should be about forty-nine.[57] This figure does not include those who are still missing and the many wounded who were taken to hospitals in Wolfheze and Oosterbeek. How many of these later died of their wounds, either in Holland or elsewhere, can not be traced.

The exact number of British losses on Ginkel Heath will most probably always remain unknown.

On Saturday, 23 September, and five days after the actual landings, the German *Ortskommandant* ordered fifty citizens of Ede to search for the remains of the British that were killed in action. A police constable was put in charge of the identification and in the woods east of the municipal timber yard along the Ede-Arnhem road a mass grave was dug.[58] In the course of the following three days thirty-five allied and eight German servicemen were buried in this provisional graveyard.

According to the list from Ede and the Roll of Honour the remains of other soldiers were buried on the spot where they were found. After the war most of them were re-buried at the Arnhem Oosterbeek War Cemetery, while two of them found their last resting place at the Algemene Begraafplaats in Ede.

The remains of all the other soldiers who were killed in the woods or on the heath, were either found much later or have to be considered as missing.

Both sides in the Battle for Ginkel Heath suffered a lot of casualties. They bear witness to the utter madness and futility of warfare. In this respect one of Middlebrook's interviews may be illustrative.

When charging a machine gun set up on a pile of logs along the Ede-Arnhem road Lieutenant Pat Mackey showed exceptional bravery, which in the end cost him his life. Private Ralph Shackleton later found his body between the trees just off the DZ. He put Lieutenant Mackey's inscribed gold ring into his mouth to prevent it from being taken by the Germans. Near the lieutenant was a dying German. The right-hand side of his head had been hit and smashed open. He was still conscious and mumbling, and when Private

The grave of Lieutenant Pat Mackey on Algemene Begraafplaats in Ede. The epitaph on the gravestone reads:

Lieutenant
. P.W.A. Mackey
of British Guyana
Parachute Regiment
Army Air Corps
18th September 1944. Age 24
"They feared no foe
with thee at hand to bless."

(PHOTO: AUTHOR)

Shackleton bent over him he put his hand out and rested it on one of Shackleton's Bren magazine pouches. The British paratrooper gave him Lieutenant Mackey's morphia and left them lying together on the grass. Shackleton later said that he still felt the futility and sadness of that moment.[59]

It is the same feeling which General Eisenhower expressed when he remarked: 'I hate war as someone who has seen its cruelty, its uselessness and its stupidity.'

After the war Lieutenant Pat Mackey was laid to rest at the Algemene Begraafplaats in Ede.

Von Tettau's push to the DZs and LZs from the west had failed and in his war diary the general noted: 'The initial successful actions by the SS *Wach Bataillon 3* had gone completely lost by the second enemy landings.'[60]

Despite the problems experienced at the landings all units of 4th Parachute Brigade quickly assembled at their RVs and within half an hour approximately seventy-five percent had reported present.[61]

At 16.15 hours the three battalions had established radio contact.[62] According to the plan of operations Hackett and his brigade were to occupy the high grounds to the north and northeast of Arnhem in order to secure the planned bridgehead against enemy attacks. Before Hackett's forces left Ginkel Heath, two staff officers of divisional headquarters in Oosterbeek arrived through the underpass of the '*Hazenpad*'. They informed Hackett of Brigadier Hicks' decision, who at that moment was acting in command of the division, that 11th Parachute Battalion was to march off to the bridge at Arnhem at the utmost speed in order to reinforce Frost's battalion, already at the bridge. It had been decided to take away Hackett's 11th Battalion because its RV at the southeastern corner of Ginkel Heath was closest to the bridge.[63] In order to maintain the battle strength of his brigade, 7 KOSB was attached to Hackett's brigade.

At about 17.00 hours 4th Parachute Brigade started moving towards Arnhem. 11th Battalion was the first to go and chose the route along the railway line to Wolfheze. From there it advanced through Wolfhezerweg and via Oosterbeek, Mariëndaal, Oosterbeek Laag Station, Klingelbeekseweg and Hulkesteinseweg to Utrechtseweg in the western part of Arnhem. En route to the bridge it managed to reach the area to the west of the St Elisabeth's Hospital (see map no. 2). Once there it was halted by the German blocking line, which was built west of the city centre. In the end the battalion would never reach the bridge.

Shortly after the departure of 11th Parachute Battalion 156 Battalion started its advance on Arnhem taking the route north of the railway line. It reached Wolfheze at about 20.00 hours that night. There the battalion was joined by the gliderborne lift, the detachment that had landed near Heelsum carrying the heavy equipment.[64] Meanwhile the German opposition got stronger and in the end the battalion was halted at Johannahoeve Farm (see map no. 2). The German defensive line at Dreijenseweg prevented a further advance. 156 Battalion was stopped far from its intended position.

After having finished securing Ginkel Heath the men of B, C and D Company 7 KOSB had a cup of tea and read the morning papers that were brought on the second lift. They were surprised to find news of the airborne landings of the previous day printed on the front pages.[65] Not much later they were joined by two platoons that were left behind in England after their gliders had crashed on the first day of the operation and which had arrived on the second lift.[66]

After a quick hot meal – the first food they had since Sunday afternoon – they started in the direction of Johannahoeve Farm at 19.00 hours. This was the LZ-L where the glider detachment carrying the Polish jeeps and anti-tank guns was to land the next morning and which was to be secured by 7 KOSB against possible German attacks.

The battalion hardly managed to reach its appointed position round midnight.

According to Beekmeijer 'they were held up by fixed gunfire'.[67] Together with the men of 156 Battalion, 7 KOSB dug in near Johannahoeve Farm which later burnt down during the fighting.

The Johannahoeve Farm position was held till the afternoon of 19 September. Under very difficult circumstances the Borderers were joined by a number of Poles who had landed in their gliders on LZ-L and had suffered heavy losses in the process.

A Company 7 KOSB left its position separated from the other companies. Without having managed to establish any contact with battalion headquarters it advanced from Planken Wambuis Café along Amsterdamseweg to Arnhem, but could not get beyond *Schweizer Höhe* (see map no. 2). There the company was forced to dig in. Until approximately Tuesday afternoon it remained completely cut off from the rest of 7 KOSB.

It was nearly dark when 10th Battalion left Ginkel Heath. The delay was caused by 133 Parachute Field Ambulance 'with its numbers of casualties', which 10th Battalion had to protect until all wounded had been carried off.[68]

The battalion advanced along the railway line in the direction of Wolfheze where it dug in for the night. During this night the battalion was equipped with its transport vehicles and anti-tank guns, which had been unloaded at LZ-X north of Heelsum. The vanguard of the battalion had advanced further down Amsterdamseweg, but it was halted near the pumping-station of the Arnhem waterworks at 03.00 hours. The British were under fire from the outposts of the Germans, which, under command of the SS, had taken up positions along Dreijenseweg. 10th Battalion was facing superior forces and because the paratroopers did not have armoured vehicles and field guns at their disposal their advance was halted on Amsterdamseweg.

Hackett's staff left Ginkel Heath at approximately 20.00 hours and spent its first night in Holland in De Buunderkamp Hotel.

At that moment nearly all the British had left Ginkel Heath. That night only a sergeant was walking around to collect stragglers and to direct them via the northern bank of the railway line to the brigade, which had advanced beyond Wolfheze railway station.

In the middle of the night part of 133 Parachute Field Ambulance, which had landed near Otterlo at approximately three miles north of Ginkel Heath, arrived on the spot where it should have landed. Along the way this detachment had grown to twenty men and was redirected to the Casualty Clearing Station, that was set up in the psychiatric hospital in Wolfheze.

Early the next morning two groups of paratroopers, who had survived the forced landing of their transport planes near Rhenen, arrived at Ginkel Heath and were also redirected to Wolfheze.

The Battle for Ginkel Heath had come to an end. For the citizens of Ede this meant the final episode of the exiting events that lasted two days, but which were not understood at the time and which caused great disappointment. In anticipation of their liberation many of them had the Dutch flag at the ready. However, this was not to be. The only thing the fighting at Ginkel Heath had left them were blouses, dresses and shorts made of parachute silk and English cigarettes taken out of containers that were hanging from some trees on De Hindenkamp. Regretfully, the colours of the national flag had to be hidden from the German occupiers again.

Wedding dress made of parachute silk (nylon).

It would not be until April 1945 before the citizens of Ede could finally hoist them.

4. Ginkel Heath, Tuesday, 19 September – Friday, 22 September 1944

In the course of Tuesday morning the Germans assembled all men of the *Wach Bataillon* who had not deserted and about eighty men reported at Simon Stevin barracks. That day the German forces in Ede were reinforced by a battalion of the *Sicherungs Regiment 42* under the command of Lieutenant Colonel Knoche. He replaced Helle as commander of operations east of Ede and his battalion was assigned Helle's task of eliminating British stragglers in the woods east of Ginkel Heath in the direction of Wolfheze.[1]

The battalion of the *Sicherungs Regiment* left for Wolfheze from the high ground east of the barracks together with two sections of the *7. Kompanie, 4. SS Panzer Grenadier Ausbildungs-und Ersatz Batail lon* from Simon Stevin barracks. North and south of the Ede-Arnhem road the columns split up and their assignment was obvi-ous, viz. to clear the heath and De Sijsselt woods and push on in an easterly direction. Thanks to the absence of any opponents the Germans acquitted themselves of their task in a most excellent way. In fact they literally followed in the footsteps of the British.

The remainder of the *Wach Bataillon* and the section of the *7. Kompanie*, which was earlier incorporated in this battalion, adopted the same 'tactics'. Meanwhile the commanding officer of the *Wach Bataillon* had removed his headquarters once again, this time to the Hotel Welgelegen near Ede Station. At approximately 07.00 hours that morning the eighty men left the barracks near the station and marched through the woods north of the railway line in an easterly direction. They were ordered to search the woods for British paratroopers and to keep the railway in German hands.[2]

Around noon one section of the *7. Kompanie* was withdrawn to guard the sheds of the work camp.

Ginkel Heath on 19 September 1944. The picture was taken by a British pilot one day after the actual landings. The white spots are parachutes. The squares on the heath are ditches dug to prevent the landing of gliders. On the 'Intelligence Map'of 1st British Airborne Division in the Airborne Museum Oosterbeek these ditches are marked in red as 'small ditches'. In the centre of the picture is Zuid Ginkel Café and bottom right the work camp 't Wijde Veld.

(PHOTO: CROWN COPYRIGHT, IN: MUNICIPAL ARCHIVES, EDE, NO. 17F912)

The southwestern edge of Ginkel Heath on 19 September 1944. The thick white line is the Utrecht-Arnhem-Ober-hausen motorway under construction. Bottom left the Utrecht-Arnhem railway line.

Following the actions directed from Ede, the commander of the *Westgruppe* ordered the *SS Ausbildungs-Ersatz Bataillon,* which was advancing from Bennekom to the Ede-Arnhem railway line, to cross the tracks and search for all remaining paratroopers.

The next morning, Wednesday 20 September, the work camp on the heath and the German positions to the east of Simon Stevin barracks were strafed by allied fighter planes.[3]
That same day the various detachments of the *Westgruppe* made slow progress in the direction of Oosterbeek. Apparently the *Wach Bataillon* was not in a hurry, because after one and a half days and having advanced for only a couple of miles, it reached Wolfheze railway station on Wednesday afternoon without having met any resistance.

On Thursday, the unit of the *7. Kompanie,* that had taken up positions east of the Simon Stevin barracks, was also ordered to look for 'stragglers' in the woods to the south of the barracks.

On Friday 22 September the work camp was cleared, as one did not expect any further British actions on the heath and that same day *7. Kompanie* was transferred to the village of Hardenberg in the eastern part of Holland.[4]

After the fighting round Arnhem had ended the supreme commander of the German *Wehrmacht* in Holland, General Christiansen, expressed his thanks to *Westgruppe Von Tettau* in a routine order in which he used the following words: 'Soldiers of the *Kampfgruppe Von Tettau!* The struggle against the 1st British Airborne Division is a glorious feat in the history of the German soldier. Under the resolute and dynamic guidance of General Von Tettau a well trained and experienced opponent was inflicted a crushing defeat.'[5]

However, these words of praise by the *General der Flieger* and former tugboat captain have to be looked at in the proper perspective. In the aftermath of the fighting on and around Ginkel Heath and in the Renkum-Heelsum area, the German forces and the Dutch SS units of *Westgruppe* did not do much more than slowly advance towards Oosterbeek, while the British paratroopers 'happened' to advance along the same route.

Once in Oosterbeek several detachments of *Westgruppe* did participate in the fighting in the western section of the perimeter, the small area round the Hartenstein Hotel, Major General Urquhart's 1st Airborne's Divisional Headquarters (see map no.2).

However, the British airborne troops were not defeated by Von Tettau's *Westgruppe*, but by the self-propelled guns, armoured vehicles and tanks of the armoured divisions of the *Ostgruppe*. The 9. *SS Panzer Division* blocked off all access roads to Arnhem city centre and the 10. *SS Panzer Division* took up positions in the Betuwe area and thus prevented the British Second Army to reach Urquhart's airborne troops on time.

5. The Significance of the Battle for Ginkel Heath

On the British side the Battle for Ginkel Heath was fought by 7th Battalion The King's Own Scottish Borderers complemented by the Advance Party of 4th Parachute Brigade and No. 3 Platoon 21st Independent Parachute Company. According to the Operational Instructions of the 1st British Airborne Division their task was the following: 'To put up outposts on the Ede-Arnhem trunk road in the vicinity of Planken Wambuis Café and to secure the arrival of the second lift on DZ-Y, Ginkel Heath'.[1]

They have performed this task most capably and successfully whilst showing the utmost dedication. Despite the quick German response they managed to hold most of their positions against increasing opposition. During the night of 17 and early morning of 18 September they were not able to prevent the Germans and Dutch SS from occupying both the north and northeasterly sections of the heath. The wooded area surrounding Ginkel Heath was simply too vast to handle for the limited number of men. Moreover, conditions on the ground made the lines of communications next to impossible. The battalion was left completely on its own and it had to do without any reinforcements from other units of 1st British Airborne Division or any air support.

In addition the Germans had the advantage of the operation taking place in the direct vicinity of their army barracks in Ede town, which enabled them to deploy the garrison within a couple of hours. At the same time troops could be brought in from elsewhere within a very short period of time.

The climax of the Battle for Ginkel Heath was 4th Parachute Brigade's drop. Thanks to the valiant actions of the airborne troops on the ground shortly before the landings, the brigade's losses were

Major General Roy E. Urquhart at the entrance of Hartenstein Hotel at Oosterbeek, 1st British Airborne Division HQ.

limited. The compliment Brigadier Hackett made to Lieutenant Colonel Payton Reid and his men after the fighting was fully deserved. They offered the protection the brigade counted on.

The actions of 7 KOSB, together with the defence of the LZs north of the Heelsum-Renkum line by the 1st Battalion The Border Regiment, caused considerable losses to Von Tettau's *Westgruppe*. Furthermore these German forces were so tied down during the first days of the Battle of Arnhem that they only could be deployed against the Oosterbeek perimeter at the last stage.

The arrival of 4th Parachute Brigade on Monday 18 September did only have a marginal influence on the further course of the fighting around Arnhem. However, this was not due to the commitment or fighting qualities of the brigade. The adverse circumstances under which the British division had to take the Arnhem road bridge were not to improve by the newly arrived paratroopers.

The only direct result of its arrival on Ginkel Heath was a change in the quantity ratio between both sides. Before the landings the Germans had the advantage, i.e. fourteen battalions on the German side as opposed to six on the British and this does not include the German tanks, artillery and heavy infantry weapons. In his book Kershaw writes: 'The combat ratio was more than two against one with an overwhelming preponderance of heavy equipments on the German side'.[2]

The German numerical superiority decreased after the landings only.

The reinforcement of the 1st British Airborne Division by 4th Parachute Brigade had a sobering and somewhat disheartening effect on the Germans. The Chief of Staff of the *9. SS Hohenstaufen Division* stated that, although the situation on the morning of 18 September was not 'rosy', the Germans were in excellent spirits to make the best of it. However, that same afternoon his optimism was tempered when he was informed about the landings on Ginkel Heath. The German asked himself: 'Because we had been sent to

Russia, we were too late in Normandy. In Arnhem we were too few! How were we to stop this elite airborne division?'3

It would soon turn out that there was no cause for this German pessimism. Although the number of British combatants increased after the landings on Ginkel Heath, right from the start of the operation on Sunday, 17 September, they had to face an enemy, which had weapons at its disposal that could not possibly be carried by any airborne division at that moment in time. This disadvantage could not be cancelled out by the arrival of 4th Parachute Brigade and besides the Germans could count on a constant flow of reinforcements.

Hackett and his 4th Parachute Brigade did contribute to upholding the perimeter at Oosterbeek for as long as was humanly possible though this contribution would have been more effective if the brigade had landed elsewhere. Ginkel Heath was no ideal DZ for two reasons. First, it was to close to Ede with its German garrison and secondly it was too far from the Arnhem road bridge, the division's target. Moreover, these disadvantages were enhanced by the fact that 4th Parachute Brigade only landed on the second day of Operation Market. The element of surprise of the airborne operation was gone after the arrival of the first lift on the previous day. This meant that both the preparation prior to the landings by 7 KOSB and the dropping itself led to a prompt reaction by the German forces that were billeted in Ede and immediate surroundings as well as by the other German troops that were put on the alert.

This implied the real danger of fierce fighting at and round the DZ at the moment on which 4th Parachute Brigade would appear above Ginkel Heath.

The success of any airborne operation largely depends on the speed with which the airborne soldiers advance on their target. Once on the ground they need their transport vehicles straightaway. However, 4th Parachute Brigade landed furthest away from the Arnhem road bridge and after having landed had to march from Ginkel

Airborne Monument 'The Eagle' on the edge of Ginkel Heath. It was designed by Mrs H. van Heuff-van Oven and made by Messrs J. Rombouts and K.van Berkel. In the background on the right is Zuid Ginkel Café. Major General R.E. Urquhart officially unveiled the monument on 19 September 1960.

Heath to Wolfheze where their rolling stock had arrived, that was carried by gliders to LZ-X north of Heelsum. Because of this precious time was lost. Especially 11th Parachute Battalion, which was to advance on the bridge as soon as possible, suffered the adverse consequences of these events. Once past Wolfheze the battalion finally had its vehicles at its disposal.[4] When it arrived at divisional headquarters at Oosterbeek, the battalion had to wait more than two hours for further orders.[5]

Hackett's other two battalions also lost much time before they actually could go into battle. 156 Battalion left the heath more than two hours after it had landed and 10th Parachute Battalion had to protect units of 133 Parachute Field Ambulance and could only leave in the course of the evening.

In order to join the rest of the division Hackett's brigade had to cover too great a distance and in the process had to advance through an area where by then heavy fighting had broken out. As a result Hackett lost the majority of his troops during the landings and the advance on Oosterbeek. In the end no more than five hundred men of his decimated 4th Parachute Brigade took part in the fighting at the Oosterbeek perimeter.

Of the various units of the 1st British Airborne Division, 4th Parachute Brigade comparatively suffered the largest number of men killed, i.e. 17.1 percent.[6]

On Tuesday evening approximately 270 men of 7th Battalion KOSB, a figure a little more than one third of the initial battle strength, reached Oosterbeek under the command of Lieutenant Colonel Payton Reid.

Regrettably, the British troops, which had been involved in the fighting on Ginkel Heath, could not do anything to improve the ackward situation of the division at the Oosterbeek perimeter. It was only a temporary reprieve.

When the advance guard of the British Second Army finally reached the south bank of the river Rhine it was too late. The fighting at the Arnhem road bridge had ended on Thursday, 21 September. The perimeter was evacuated in the night of 25 and early morning of 26 September.[7] The survivors of the Battle of Arnhem were ferried across the Rhine east of Driel or tried to swim to the other riverbank, leaving hundreds of killed and wounded behind. In a conversation between Churchill and Eisenhower during the preparations of the Normandy landings, the British Prime Minister told the Supreme Allied Commander: 'If you manage to establish a bridgehead from the river Seine estuary to Cherbourg and the Brittany peninsula by winter and if you have put thirty-six divisions ashore, I shall consider this a victory. If you have also taken Le

Havre, I shall call it a decisive one.' Eisenhower answered: 'We shall be at the Rhine round Christmas'.[8] 'At the Rhine' indeed, but not across.

Notes

INTRODUCTION

1. Georg Tessin, *Verbände und Truppen der deutschen Wehrmacht und Waffen-SS im Zweiten Weltkrieg 1939-1945*, 16er Band, Teil 4, Besetzte Gebiete Nord/West/Süd, Osnabrück, 1997.

   In this summary the following German units are mentioned that were involved in the fighting on Ginkel Heath:

   - *SS-Panzer Grenadier Ausbildungs-und Ersatz Bataillon 4* (Trainings and Reserve Battalion, quartered in Simon Stevin barracks in Ede):
     (Georg Tessin, 16er Band, Teil 4, 211; 2er Band, 78, 276);

   - *20. Schiffs-Stamm-Abteilung* (a unit of the coastal defences, quartered at Maurits and Johan W. Friso barracks in Ede):
     (Georg Tessin, 16er Band, Teil 4, 191; 2er Band: Kriegsmarine 131; 4er Band, 147).

   - *SS-Wach Bataillon 3*, formerly SS-Wach Bataillon Nordwest. Carried out guard duties at the Amersfoort concentration camp since 15 April 1944 :
     (Georg Tessin, 16er Band, Teil 4, 211).

1. ALLIED STRATEGY AFTER THE NORMANDY LANDINGS

1. B.L. Montgomery, *Normandy to the Baltic*, London, 1947, p. 136. He writes: 'We should strike on the least likely line from the enemy's point of view'.

   The Germans disputed the direction of the next allied advance. The German Field Marshal Model, supreme commander *Heeresgruppe B*, thought he was safe north of the great rivers in Holland and therefore established his headquarters at the Tafelberg Hotel inOosterbeek. On 15 September 1944 he received in this hotel Rauter, SS Chief cum Chief of Police in occupied Holland. Model told his guest that he did not expect any airborne landings in Holland. In his opinion the Allies would not deploy airborne forces before having reached the river Rhine at Düsseldorf to force open a bridgehead.

Two days after the talks with Rauter, Model was having lunch at his headquarters when the first British paratroopers landed west of Oosterbeek. (C. Bauer, *Verrassing in het kwadraat* (= consummate surprise), in: *Bericht van de Tweede Wereldoorlog* (= report from World War II), No. 75, volume 5, Amsterdam, 1971, p. 2083). Contrary to Model the German military intelligence staff did consider an allied advance to the north. Taken the positions of the allied armies a combined ground and airborne attack was deemed a real possibility. In several scripts Eindhoven, Arnhem, the IJsselmeer and Venlo-Wesel were mentioned as possible lines of attack. On 16 September the intelligence staff of *Heeresgruppe-B* indicated that an allied push from positions east of Antwerp to the 'Zuiderzee' (IJsselmeer) had to be taken into account. (*Anlageband Heeresgruppe-B, Ic Meldungen*, 1/9/44-30/9/44, *Ic- Abendmeldung* AOK15, 16/9/1944, *Ic-185*).

The German Supreme Command speculated on an allied offensive in the direction of Wesel, Münster or Lünen. The information furnished by double agent Lindemans, aka King Kong, that allied paratroopers would probably land near Eindhoven on 16 September, was disregarded. Tactically, Operation Market Garden was a complete surprise. (C. Klep and B. Schoenmaker, *De bevrijding van Nederland 1944-1945. Oorlog op de flank*. (= The Liberation of The Netherlands 1944-1945. War on the Flank), 's-Gravenhage, 1995, pp. 117-118).

With regard to the part Lindemans played in all this, Dutch historian Mr Lou de Jong was outspoken in his conclusion that the former actually betrayed Arnhem during an interview with the Gestapo in Driebergen on 15 September.

However, in his book Mr De Jong confirms that the betrayal did not have any effect on the course of the war. (L. de Jong, *Het Koninkrijk der Nederlanden in de Tweede Wereldoorlog* (= The Kingdom of The Netherlands during World War II), part 10A, *Het laatste jaar I* (= The final year I), 1e helft, 's-Gravenhage, 1980, p. 427).

2. B.L. Montgomery, *Memoires,* (= Memoirs) 4th ed. , Amsterdam, s.a., p. 273. In this book Montgomery calls his 'masterplan' a 'reverse *Von Schlieffen* plan'. He referred to a plan of 1905, which was devised by the Chief of Staff of the Imperial German Army Von Schlieffen. It was designed for a German attack on France. In order to get round the French system of fortresses, that stretched out from Verdun to Belfort on the French eastern border, the German armies were to outflank these defences through Holland and Belgium and to advance through northern France. The French city of Metz was to act as a sort of pivotal point.

After 1930 these French defences were extended into what later became known as the Maginot line. With the exception of some major changes the plan was used both in 1914 and 1940 for the German invasion of France.

3. C. Klep and B. Schoenmaker, *De bevrijding van Nederland 1944-1945. Oorlog op de flank* (= The Liberation of The Netherlands 1944-1945. War on the Flank), 's-Gravenhage, 1995, p. 98.
4. Dwight D. Eisenhower, *Crusade in Europe*, New York, 1952, p. 438.
5. Alistair Horne, *Monty, The Lonely Leader, 1944-1945*, New York, 1994, p. 284.
6. A.D. Harvey, *Arnhem*, London, 2001, pp. 18-19.
7. Dwight D. Eisenhower, pp. 344-345. According to some critics Eisenhower's remark about a 'pencillike thrust' did not do justice to Montgomery's original plan, which provided for a combined allied advance to the north by Montgomery's own 21st British Army Group and the 12th US Army Group of General Omar Bradley, totalling forty divisions.(Alistair Horne, pp. 282-283).
   The question whether such an operation can still be labelled as a 'pencillike thrust' does not alter the fact that Eisenhower was opposed to an advance over a small front and the subsequent problems of supplying his forces.
8. Stephen E. Ambrose, *The Supreme Commander: The War Years of General Dwight D. Eisenhower*, London, 1971, pp. 515-519.
9. Norman Gelb, *Ike & Monty. Generals at War*, New York, 1994, p. 360. All the same, many staff officers within the Allied Supreme Command found it curious that a usually cautious strategist like Montgomery came up with this most audacious plan and that it was accepted by Eisenhower who was a great champion of a 'broad front' strategy. There has been a lot of speculation about the reason of the allied supreme commander's go-ahead. According to Richard Lamb Eisenhower was wrongly informed by his intelligence staff with regard to the speed with which the Germans reinforced their front against Montgomery's 21st Army Group. Lamb suggests that Eisenhower would probably have taken another decision if he had realised that the Germans were reinforcing so quickly. (Richard Lamb, *Montgomery in Europe, 1943-1945. Success or Failure?*, London, 1983, p. 217).
   David Irving suggests that Eisenhower did agree in order to make an end to Montgomery's nagging. Both commanders profoundly disagreed about which strategy to pursue. Eisenhower had made it absolutely clear that he did not fancy a 'pencillike thrust' towards the Ruhr area and Berlin. In spite of this the British Field Marshal tried to

force his 'masterplan' through during a period of several weeks. According to Irving, Eisenhower most probably reasoned that if the gamble of Market Garden should succeed, the glory was to be shared by both men, while a failure 'would silence Montgomery for some time'. (David Irving, *The War between the Generals*, New York, 1981, p. 281).

These are only attempts to clarify the actual facts. Fact is that Eisenhower, as supreme commander, not only had to deal with the military situation, but also with the public opinion in both the United States and England in which national sentiments played a major role. At the same time he also had to satisfy some extremely ambitious seconds in command which he once called his 'prima donnas'.

According to Omar Bradley, the commanding officer of the 12th US Army Group, Eisenhower made his greatest tactical error of the whole war by giving in to Montgomery's wishes. Market Garden was an offensive in the wrong direction and it would have been well-advised to order the advance of both Hodges' 1st US Army and Patton's 3rd US Army to the east. These could have reached a position on the Rhine from where it would have been strategically easier to prepare for the final assault on Germany than the British would have had if Operation Market Garden had been a success. (Omar N. Bradley, *A General's Life*, New York, 1983, p. 333).

10. Eric Larrabee, *Commander in Chief. Franklin Delano Roosevelt, His Lieutenants & Their War*, London, 1987, p. 483.

11. A.D. Harvey, p. 15.

12. B.L. Montgomery, *Normandy to the Baltic*, pp. 136-139.

13. B.L. Montgomery, *Memoires*, p. 283.

14. Richard Lamb, *Montgomery in Europe 1943-1945. Success or Failure?*, London, 1983, p. 214.

'The precision and destructive power of the 'weapons of retaliation' (the V1 and V2 rockets) soon turned out to be too limited to effectively change the military strategy.

Furthermore, it could reasonably be expected that the quick allied advance would eliminate their threat in due course.'(C. Klep and B. Schoenmaker, p. 98).

Montgomery's obsession with the Ruhr area also resulted in the fact that he did not bother to occupy the seaway to Antwerp after this Belgian port had been taken by the Allies on 4 September. In order to supply the allied forces full control of the Westerschelde river was of decisive importance. More than once Eisenhower urged Montgomery to make the port of Antwerp suitable for the transport of supplies and troops as soon as possible, but the British Field Marshal only had eyes for his own 'masterplan'. Moreover, after having taken Antwerp, he ordered his troops to stop their advance and so failed to push on to Woensdrecht enabling the German 15th Army to escape from Zuid-Beveland, one of the islands in the province of Zeeland. As a result between eighty-two and eighty-six thousand German forces together with 530 to 616 field guns managed to retreat into the province of Brabant, where Montgomery would meet them later on. (A.D. Harvey, p. 22).

15. David Irving, *The War between the Generals*, New York, 1981, pp. 279-280.

2. SUNDAY, 17 SEPTEMBER 1944: D-DAY

1. Allied Expeditionary Air Force, Daily Int/Ops Summary no. 242, Section 'A', General Information, Para I Overlord, From information received up to 05.00 hours 18 Sept. 1944, pp. 1, 3.
2. John C. Warren, *Airborne Operations in World War II, European Theater, USAF Historical Studies*, no. 97, USAF Historical Division, Research Studies Institute, Air University, September 1956, p. 100.
3. AEAF, 4.
   Michael J.F. Bowyer, *2 Group RAF, A complete History, 1936-1945*, p. 396.
4. V. Lagerweij and G. Plekkeringa, *Ede 1940-1945*, Barneveld, 1985, p. 41.
5. Labahn, *Gefechtsbericht der 7. (Stamm) Kompanie für die Zeit vom 17.9 bis 26.9.44, 1* (= war diary of 7. *Stammkompanie* for the period of 17 till 26 September 1944) in: *Map 258, 2e afd. Documentatie Bevrijding Veluwe (1)*, Market Garden, *gemeentearchief Ede* (File No. 258, 2nd Dept. Documentation Liberation of the Veluwe (1), Municipal Archives, Ede).
   NB: The spelling of the word Beeckman barracks is based on the original drawings at the Municipal Archives, Ede.
6. Th. A. Boeree, *Aantekeningen betreffende de Slag om Arnhem* (= notes with regard to the Battle of Arnhem), pp. 8, 26, in: File No. 259, Market Garden, Municipal Archives, Ede.
7. R.E. Urquhart, *De Slag om Arnhem* (= The Battle of Arnhem), 2nd ed., Leiden, 1958, pp. 47-48.
8. AEAF, 1.
9. *By Air to Battle, The official Account of the British Airborne Divisions*, London, 1945, p. 98.
10. R.E. Urquhart, 1958, p. 19.
11. Christopher Hibbert, *Arnhem, 17-26 September 1944*, Baarn, 1982, p. 37.
12. R.E. Urquhart, p. 208.

13. Quoted from the war diary of Major J.A. Hibbert in: *De Zwarte Herfst; Arnhem 1944* (= Black Autumn; Arnhem 1944) by Messrs C.A. Dekkers and L.P.J. Vroemen, Weesp, 1984, p. 55.
14. Martin Middlebrook, *Arnhem. Ooggetuigen van de Slag om Arnhem, 17-26 september 1944* (= Arnhem. Eyewitnesses to the Battle of Arnhem, 17-26 September 1944), Baarn, 1994, pp. 108-112.
15. James M. Gavin, *Op naar Berlijn (On to Berlin)*, Amsterdam, 1980, p. 186.
    According to Harvey the distance between the DZs and LZs and the Arnhem road bridge has had less influence on the failure at Arnhem than the decision to direct only part of the British forces to the bridge on the first day. (A.D. Harvey, pp. 180-181).
    It is hardly possible to pinpoint which of these details did influence the final defeat at the most. It is rather a sum of mistakes on the British side to which the accidental presence of heavily armoured Germans must be added. The difference in weaponry was the main reason why the British and Polish airborne forces did not stand a chance right from the start.
16. The article by C. Wilmot and entitled 'Werd Montgomery's plan verraden?' (= 'Was Montgomery's plan betrayed?') appeared in the *Algemeen Dagblad* (a Dutch national newspaper) of the 16th of September, 1950.
17. B.L. Montgomery, *Memoires*, p. 307.
18. R. Payton Reid, Personal Account Operations 7th Bn KOSB, File No. 54-2, p.1, R.N. Sigmond archives.
19. R.N. Sigmond, *Off at Last, An Illustrated History of the 7th (Galloway) Battalion The King's Own Scottish Borderers, 1939-1945*. From Official Records and Personal Accounts of Members of the Battalion, Ede, 1997, p. 54.
20. R.E. Urquhart, p. 23.
21. Dwight D. Eisenhower, *Eisenhower's Own Story of the War. The Complete Report by the Supreme Commander on the War in Europe from the Day of Invasion to the Day of Victory*, New York, 1946, p. 67.
    In the Dutch translation of Eisenhower's report (Dwight D. Eisenhower, *Van Invasie tot Victorie*, Amsterdam, s.a.) page 179 reads as follows: 'The 1st British Airborne Division heroically resisted a superior force that was equipped with a number of tanks the presence of which had not been estimated by my intelligence staff.' This sentence has a remarkable footnote, which reads as follows:'The printed version of Eisenhower's report probably contains an error. It reads "the presence of which had been estimated by my intelligence staff". This probably

should read "had not been estimated". Apparently the translator acted on his own and made a substantial alteration in the text of the report.

The likely reason for this error is that the translator could not believe that the presence of both German SS armoured divisions in the Arnhem area was known at the allied headquarters which still issued the order to proceed.

22. H. Bollen, *Corridor naar de Rijn, Operatie Market Garden September 1944* (= Corridor to the Rhine, Operation Market Garden, September 1944), Zutphen, 1988, p. 23.
23. Peter Harclerode, *Arnhem, A Tragedy of Errors*, London, 1994, p. 38.
24. David Eisenhower, *Eisenhower: At War 1943-1945*, New York, 1986, p. 470.
25. Cornelius Ryan, *Een brug te ver* (*A Bridge Too Far*), Bussum, 1974, pp. 110-111.
   C. Klep and B. Schoenmaker, p. 114.
26. *Gefechtsbericht der SS Pz. Gren. Ausb. u. Ers. Btl. 16 über die Kämpfe gegen die 1. Brit. Fallschirmjäger Div. in der Zeit von 17.9 – 7.10.1944 im Raume Arnheim, 6, (Rapport Krafft)*, (= war diary of the SS *Ausbildungs- und Ersatz Bataillon 16* of the engagements with 1st British Airborne Division between 17 September and 7 October 1944). Boeree collection, Municipal Archives, Arnhem.
27. A.D. Harvey, p. 189.
28. R. Brammall, *The Tenth, a Record of the 10th Battalion, the Parachute Regiment*, London, 1965, p. 45.
29. *Tagesbefehl Heeresgruppe B, 28-9-1944, in: Abschnitt 11, 16 September – 10 Oktober 1944* (= Order of the day Army Group B, 28 September 1944), p. 424; in: File No. 259, Market Garden, Municipal Archives, Ede.
30. R.E. Urquhart, p. 57.
31. Cornelius Ryan, pp. 230, 231.
   Interviews in: *Ryan Papers*, Ohio State University, Athens, Ohio.
32. Ibid, pp. 204, 205, 231.
   In an article in *NRC Handelsblad* (Dutch national newspaper) of 20 September 1986 A. Korthals Altes claims that it emerged from a German document that the Germans only seized an order of the day for 101st US Airborne Division. However, Bollen claims that as late as 1988 this document had never turned up. (H. Bollen, pp. 44-45).
   See also: Karel Margry, *Operation Market Garden - Then and Now*, London, 2002, p. 173.
33. C. Bauer and Th. A. Boeree, *De Slag bij Arnhem. De mythe van het verraad weerlegd.*(= The Battle of Arnhem, the myth of treason refuted), Amsterdam and Brussels, 1964, p. 64.

34. 1 Airborne Division. Report on Operation 'Market', s.a., Part V, Detailed Reports by Arms other than Infantry, Annexure Q, Intelligence Summary No. 4 dated 22 September 1944.
35. H. von Tettau, *Einsatz des Stabes Von Tettau in Holland, Sept. – Okt. 1944* (= War Diary Division Von Tettau in Holland, Sept. – Oct. 1944), MS # P-187, p. 3, Airborne Museum Hartenstein Archives, Oosterbeek.
36. C. Bauer and Th.A. Boeree, pp. 63, 57.
37. H. von Tettau, pp. 25, 3.
38. E.R.E. Carter, *Nine Days at Arnhem, Personal Account Operations B Coy no. 6 Platoon, 7th Bn KOSB*, p. 6, R.N. Sigmond archives.
39. 1 Airborne Division. Report on Operation 'Market', s.a., Part IV, Annexure D, Operations Instructions, 1 Para Bde, 1 Topography.
40. This work camp was built for the unemployed youth of Ede. It was officially opened on 13 May 1935 and consisted of six sheds. Two of these were used for sleeping and as living quarters. The others housed the camp leader and his wife, and were used as kitchen, dining and recreation rooms.

    After working hours, the boys could read, study, play sports and take a first aid course. (From an article in the *Edesche Courant*, a local newspaper, dated 11 May 1935).

    During World War II the camp housed labourers, who were working on the '*Hazenpad*'.

    The Germans had the intention to use this trunk road for the quick displacement of their forces from the German border to The Hague, and which they needed for the planned invasion of England. After the defeat of the *Luftwaffe* in the Battle of Britain the construction of this road was stopped in 1942.

    The Germans did not want to take the risk of the Allies gratefully using it during an eventual advance on Germany. Besides, the Germans could make better use of the building material elsewhere. (Th.A. Boeree, *The History of 7th Bn KOSB in the Battle of Arnhem*, s.a., p. 24, Boeree collection, Municipal Archives, Arnhem).
41. G.C. Gourlay, *Personal Account Operations D Coy, 7th Bn KOSB*, p. 4, R.N. Sigmond archives.
42. R.N. Sigmond, p. 61.
43. War Diary, 7th (Galloway) Bn KOSB; Public Record Office, WO 171/1323, p. 5.
44. One tends to put the blame for the inadequate communications on Divisional Signals. Lewis L. Golden has proven that already during field manoeuvres it had turned out that the proper functioning of the available radio sets strongly depended on local ground conditions.

(Lewis L. Golden, *Echoes from Arnhem*, London, 1984).
However, the same radio sets proved serviceable under other ground conditions. The British, who remained on Ginkel Heath after the fighting as well as members of the Dutch resistance, realised this only too well. A couple of days after the fighting had stopped the first British airborne soldiers were taken to the sheepfold of Gijs Janssen on Zecksteeg in Lunteren, where they were hidden from the Germans. One of them said that he had had to leave his set in the woods near the heath. He indicated the exact spot on an ordnance survey map after which a member of the Ede branch of the *Binnenlandse Strijdkrachten* (= Dutch Interior Forces), together with a colleague, entered De Sijssell woods via the first level crossing on the Ede-Arnhem railway line at signal box 19A. There they took fright at the sight of a German who held his rifle pointed at them. When they came closer, the man turned out to be dead. The radio set lay behind him on the ground. They picked it up and took it back to the sheepfold.
During the night of 22 and early morning of 23 October 1944 it rendered excellent services during the spectacular escape of 120 British airborne troops, ten British and American pilots, two Russians and fifteen Dutchmen via Renkum to liberated territory. This was called Operation Pegasus 1.

45. A. Beekmeijer, Letter to the Commission of Military Insignia, The Hague, 6 January 1950, in: File No. 259, Market Garden, Public Archives, Ede. Arie Beekmeijer served with No. 2 (Dutch) Troop No. 10 (Inter Allied) Commando and during the Battle of Arnhem was seconded to 7 KOSB with the special task of interrogating prisoners of war to get as much information as possible. Contrary to the men of the 1st British Airborne Division he did not wear the maroon beret, but the green one with the Dutch lion emblem worn by Dutch commandos. On his battledress he wore the Combined Operations shoulder pads. (R.N. Sigmond, p. 57).

46. S. Carr, *Personal Account Operations 10th Bn 4th Para Bde, Advance Party*, p. 5, Airborne Museum Hartenstein Archives, Oosterbeek.

47. Th.A. Boeree, The Battle of Arnhem, *Aantekeningen betreffende de Slag om Arnhem* (= notes with regard to the Battle of Arnhem), p. 57, in: File no. 259, Market Garden, Municipal Archives, Ede.

48. Labahn, p. 1. In his book 'De Slag bij Arnhem' (= *The Battle of Arnhem*) Boeree writes the following: 'Out of fear for an uprising by illegals Labahn had already barricaded himself in his barracks for a couple of days. He did not even dare to show himself that Sunday or send out reconnaissance units. (Th.A. Boeree, *De Slag bij Arnhem*, Ede, s.a., p.16.)

However, the *Gefechtsbericht* (= war diary) indicates that the Germans already took up positions on Sunday afternoon and sent out reconnaissance units later that same day.

49. Ibid., 1.
50. NCOs and other ranks of 20. *Schiff-Stamm-Abteilung* were quartered in Maurits and Johan Willem Friso barracks in Ede, while the officers were billeted in the Barbara Foundation. The detachment was part of the *Kriegsmarine* (German Navy) and the Barbara Foundation probably had a direct telephone connection with the German Navy headquarters in Hamburg. The Ede branch of the Dutch Interior Forces was very interested in disconnecting this line. A few days after the landings on Ginkel Heath, two citizens of Ede went to a spot east of Zuid Ginkel Café, where they put up the well-known tent used by the Dutch telephone company, when digging holes to repare telephone lines. Shortly before they were to cut the cable a couple of German soldiers turned up and took a rest close to the tent. The sabotage of the line was foiled and a second chance never occurred.
51. Labahn, p. 2.
52. R.N. Sigmond, p. 58.
53. Labahn, pp. 1, 3.
54. C. Bauer and Th.A. Boeree, p. 65.
55. H. Bollen, p. 79.
56. Labahn, p. 4.
57. *Roll of Honour*, compiled by J. Hey. Publ. by The Society of Friends of the Airborne Museum Oosterbeek, 4th ed., 1999, Appendix 'A', p. 94, Mass grave at Amsterdamseweg and other locations in relation to Ginkel Heath.
58. H. von Tettau, p. 4.

3. MONDAY, 18 SEPTEMBER 1944 : 'D + 1'
1. H. von Tettau, pp., 4, 6.
2. War Diary 7th (Galloway) Bn KOSB, p. 5.
3. R. Payton Reid, p. 1.
4. Police headquarters Utrecht. Subcommittee War Crimes Utrecht, Official Report following statements by the former commanding officer SS *Wach Bataillon* etc. with regard to the Battle of Arnhem, Bureau-DC, code no. 586/25, p.8.
5. Current Reports from Overseas No. 69, Section 1 – Operations by an Airlanding Battalion in the Battle for the Arnhem Bridgehead, pp. 2, 3; in: File No. 258, Market Garden, Municipal Archives, Ede,

6. R. Payton Reid, p. 2.
7. R.N. Sigmond, p. 62.
8. First In Pathfinders Report, The Company War Diary, p. 99; in: File No. 259, Market Garden, Municipal Archives, Ede.
9. S. Carr, p. 6.
10. E.R.E. Carter, pp. 9, 10.
11. M.B. Forman, *Personal Account Operations B Coy, 7th Bn KOSB*, pp. 1, 2, R.N. Sigmond archives.
12. R. Brammall, p. 52.
13. Ibid, p. 50. In his *Diary* Brigadier Hackett, commanding officer 4th Parachute Brigade, states that he was informed of approximately fifty German fighter planes appearing over the DZ at the time he was supposed to land. (J.W. Hackett, *Diary 4th Para Bde Appendix C*, in: Ref. Maps-Holland GsGs 4427-1/25,000-sheets Ginkel & Arnhem, Public Record Office, London, WO 171/594, 1).
This is also mentioned in other summaries and records (see Brammall and Waddy). However, there is no mention of an air attack by Messerschmitts on the British positions on and around Ginkel Heath in any war diary of 7 KOSB. Such an attack would have been very risky for the Germans on the ground and the *Lufwaffe* most probably strafed the DZs and LZs, which were used the previous day.
14. E.R.E. Carter, pp. 11, 12.
15. G.M. Dinwiddie, *Personal Account Operations C Coy, 7th Bn KOSB*, R.N. Sigmond archives.
16. R. Payton Reid, p. 2.
17. Th.A. Boeree, *De Slag bij Arnhem* (the Battle of Arnhem), Ede, s.a., p. 30.
18. John C. Warren, p. 125.
19. Martin Middlebrook, p. 230.
20. R. Brammall, p. 50.
21. Martin Middlebrook, p. 235.
22. John C. Warren, p. 125.
23. R. Payton Reid, p. 2.
24. Labahn, p. 3.
25. Christopher Hibbert, p. 119.
26. Robert J. Kershaw, *It Never Snows in September. The German View of Market Garden and the Battle of Arnhem September 1944*, Ramsbury, 1990, p. 160.
27. Martin Middlebrook, p. 241.
28. Th.A. Boeree, *The History of 7th Battalion KOSB in the Battle of Arnhem*, s.a., p. 48, in: File No. 258, Market Garden, Municipal Archives, Ede.
29. Martin Middlebrook, p. 240.

30. N. Cherry, *Red Berets and Red Crosses, The Story of the Medical Services in the 1st Airborne Division in WW II*, Renkum, 1999, p. 96.
31. Ibid., p. 95.
32. Martin Middlebrook, p. 236. During the Battle of Arnhem 1st British Airborne Division used eighty-two carrier-pigeons. Most of these birds were carried in containers and some in cylinders (see illustration). Fourteen pigeons returned to Engeland of which only three carried a message. The most famous bird was called William of Orange, which was released at the Rhine bridge at 19 September. At first it stayed put on a rooftop nearby, but after a short burst from a sten gun, it reached England within four and a half hours. It later received the Dicken Medal, i.e. the Victoria Cross for animals. (Supplement to Newsletter No. 10, Friends of the Airborne Museum at Oosterbeek).
The Germans also used carrier-pigeons. Their pigeonry happened to be in the park near the Hartenstein Hotel. During the first two days of the battle messages, carried by the 'German' birds, were immediately handed over to British divisional intelligence. (1 Airborne Division, Report on Operation Market, s.a., Part V, Annexure T, Index H, Pigeons).
33. Th.A. Boeree, *The Battle of Arnhem*, p. 139.
34. Ibid., p. 140.
35. J. Waddy, *A Tour of the Arnhem Battlefields*, Barnsley, 1999, p. 102.
36. A. Beekmeijer, Letter.
37. Police headquarters Utrecht. War Crimes Bureau, Official Report, pp. 6, 17.
38 Labahn, p. 4.
39. Ibid., p. 4.
Report by Public Works Department, Ede dated 13 April 1948, in: Municipal Archives, Ede.
40. *By Air to Battle*, pp. 109, 111.
41. John C. Warren, p. 126.
42. Th.A. Boeree, *The History of 7th Battalion KOSB*, p. 32.
43. R. Brammall, pp. 52, 53.
44. Th.A. Boeree, Aantekeningen, (= *Notes*), p.130.
45. J. Waddy, p. 100.
46. First In Pathfinders Report, p. 100.
47. J.W. Hackett, Diary 4th Para Bde, Appendix C, in: Ref. Maps-Holland GsGs 4427-1/25,000-sheets Ginkel & Arnhem, Public Record Office, London, WO 171/594, p. 1.
48. 1. Airborne Division, Report on Operation Market, s.a., Part IV, Annexure 0.2, 1 Airlanding Brigade Operation Market.

49. Th.A. Boeree, *The History of 7th Battalion* KOSB, p. 32.
50. C. Bauer and Th.A. Boeree, p. 180.
51. Geoffrey Powell, *De verloren slag. De bruggen naar Arnhem 1944 (The Devil's Birthday)*, Arnhem, 1989, p. 105.
52. N. Cherry, p. 95.
53. *By Air to Battle*, p. 108.
54. J. Waddy, p. 100.
55. *Roll of Honour*, 1999.
56. Martin Middlebrook, p. 241.
57. Invoice from Ede undertaker Messrs Jansen-Boeve, Municipal Archives, Ede.
A.W. Kalt, List of bodies in mass grave Ede-Arnhem trunk road in Municipal Archives, Arnhem.
Five bodies on the list belonged to an American aircrew, which perished after their plane went down over Planken Wambuis. The other thirty were killed during the fighting on Ginkel Heath. According to the *Roll of Honour* nineteen British bodies were buried on the spot. This brings the total number of British killed during the fighting near Ede to forty-nine. The actual number must be higher, but will most probably never be determined.
58. V. Lagerweij and G. Plekkeringa, p. 39.
The British dead were transported to a provisional mass grave by the Ede undertaker Messrs Jansen & Boeve using horse and wagon and some carts and a wagon furnished by the livery stable of Messrs H. van Loo from Maanderweg in Ede. The grooms were well paid by the Germans. They could also keep the cigarettes they found. On the floor of the wagons was a layer of straw and any handguns, which were found, were hidden under the straw and later handed over to members of the Ede resistance movement. A number of hand-grenades and weapons were buried near the mass grave, but later turned out to be unserviceable.
59. Martin Middlebrook, p. 237.
60. H. von Tettau, p. 6.
61. J. Waddy, p. 100.
62. J.W. Hackett, p. 1.
63. R.F. Urquhart, p. 90.
64. Report 156 Para Battalion of the 4th Para Brigade, in: File No. 258, Market Garden, Municipal Archives, Ede.
65. E.R.E. Carter, p. 13.
66. War Diary, 7th Bn KOSB, p. 7.
67. A. Beekmeijer, Letter.
68. J. Waddy, p. 102.

4. GINKEL HEATH, TUESDAY, 19 SEPTEMBER – FRIDAY, 22 SEPTEMBER 1944

1. Labahn, p. 4.
2. Police headquarters Utrecht, War Crimes Bureau, Official Report, p. 13.
3. Labahn, p. 4.
4. Ibid., pp. 4, 5.
5. H.von Tettau, pp. 35, 36.

5. THE SIGNIFICANCE OF THE BATTLE FOR GINKEL HEATH

1. R.E. Urquhart, p. 223.
2. R. Kershaw, p. 156.
3. Ibid., pp. 163, 164.
4. C. Bauer and Th.A. Boeree, p. 170.
5. A.D. Harvey, pp. 101, 102.
6. Martin Middlebrook, pp. 282, 325, 439.
7. Montgomery's 'corridor established by the airborne carpet' (B.L. Montgomery, *Normandy to the Baltic*, p.137), which was to be 'rolled' out by the airborne divisions for the advance of the British Second Army enabling it to cross the great rivers had failed. Instead of a 'carpet' Boeree uses the wording 'three small rugs'. The first was neatly put in place near Grave, the second across the river Waal at Nijmegen had still to be laid down upon arrival of the Second Army and the third, near Arnhem got lost in the process. (Th.A. Boeree, Aantekeningen, (= *Notes)*, p.5).
   In the end Operation Market Garden only yielded little territorial gain except for a little bulge of nineteen by fifty miles to the north. The allied forces suffered a lot of casualties. According to the American General Bradley '17.000 Allies killed, wounded or missing. This was far more than we suffered on D-Day in Normandy.' (Omar N. Bradley, *A General's Life*, New York, 1983, p. 332).
8. C. Wilmot, *De strijd om Europa* (The Battle for Europe), Brussels, 1952, pp. 179, 180.

Maps

Acknowledgements

I am most grateful to Drs. A. Groeneweg OBE, vice-chairman of the Airborne Museum Oosterbeek Foundation, Dr. J. Korsloot, staff member of the Airborne Museum Oosterbeek, Messrs H. Timmerman, R.M. Gerritsen and G. Maassen of the Society of Friends of the Airborne Museum Oosterbeek, the late Mr H.W.J.A. Wildenburg, staff member of the Ede branch of the Dutch Interior Forces for their indispensable assistance rendered in composing this book and the article that formed its basis. Each page reflects their exceptional expertise and some of them also assisted in the selection of the appropriate illustrations.

Also deserving my particular thanks are Mrs Janice I. Mullin of the Imperial War Museum in London, Mr J.G. Hartgers and Drs. D. List of the Museum of the Society of 'Old Ede', Mr A. Schoonderbeek and staff members of the Municipal Archives in Arnhem, the staff members of the Municipal Archives in Ede, of the *Nederlands Instituut voor Oorlogsdocumentatie* (Netherlands Institute for War Documentation) in Amsterdam and of the *Instituut voor Militaire Geschiedenis van de Koninklijke Landmacht* (Institute for Military History of the Royal Dutch Army) in The Hague.

I am especially grateful to Mr R.N. Sigmond of Renkum for the most pleasant cooperation and the liberal use of his personal archives. His knowledge and collection of data and pictures of 7 KOSB are an inexhaustible source of information, which he used for his book on the history of the battalion, that was published in 1997. I am very pleased to have been allowed to peruse his collection of official documents and personal accounts from veterans of the battalion. It is the oral and written history of those who participated in the fighting on Ginkel Heath that gives an extra dimension to this very special episode in the history of warfare.

Register

(Arnhem, Ede and Ginkel Heath are not included in this register)